Bugler & C
of the Rifles

Bugler & Officer of the Rifles

A Ranker & Officer of the 95th (Rifles)
During the Peninsular & Waterloo
Campaigns of the Napoleonic Wars

Bugler William Green
&
Harry Smith

Bugler & Officer of the Rifles A Ranker & Officer of the 95th (Rifles) During the Peninsular & Waterloo Campaigns of the Napoleonic Wars

Published by Leonaur Ltd

First Edition

Copyright © 2005 Leonaur Ltd

ISBN (10 digit): 1-84677-032-7 (hardcover)
ISBN (13 digit): 978-1-84677-032-6 (hardcover)

ISBN (10 digit): 1-84677-020-3 (softcover)
ISBN (13 digit): 978-1-84677-020-3 (softcover)

http://www.leonaur.com

Publisher's Notes

In the interests of authenticity, the spellings, grammar and place names used have been retained from the original editions.

The opinions of the authors represent a view of events in which he was a participant related from his own perspective, as such the text is relevant as an historical document.

The views expressed in this book are not necessarily those of the publisher.

Contents

Bugler William Green   9

Harry Smith   87

Bugler William Green

The Personal Experiences of
Rifleman & Bugler William "Bill" Green
of the 95th (Rifles) in the Peninsular Campaign
of the Napoleonic Wars

Chapter 1

I was born in the parish of Lutterworth, in the County of Leicester, on the 7th day of June, in the year 1784.

Having a disposition to ramble, I enlisted into the Leicester Militia, in the month of June, 1803, at the age of 19, but not content with my station, I volunteered into the old 95th, or what is now termed the Rifle Brigade, on the 18th of April, 1805, at Canterbury, in the County of Kent, with about 150 of my comrades.

Having completed my rifle drill, five companies were ordered on foreign service. An expedition was fitted out for Germany, composed of 20,000 British troops, under the command of General Donn, to check the French army in Low Germany.

We embarked at Ramsgate the latter end of October, 1805; and sailed on the 5th of November, when we bid adieu to the white cliffs of Britain. We had a pleasant passage 14 days, and then a dreadful storm arose. Three or four vessels were lost, and all hands perished; others were wrecked on the French coast, and some vessels were driven back to England. The storm continued two days and one night. A vessel ran foul of our ship in the night, and did us much damage; and we expected no other than a watery grave. The coppers were washed overboard, and many other things; but through mercy, our lives were all spared.

When daylight appeared we saw the Island of Heligoland; and on the 19th of November, we landed at a place called Cook's Haven, in Low Germany; when I heard a language we did not understand. We marched up the country to the city of Bremen, and stayed there a short time. The people were very kind to us. We were quartered on rich and poor. Tobacco was only 4d. per lb; brandy 7d. per quart; and other things cheap in proportion. We then marched further up the country to a city called Aldenburg, near the borders of Holland; but did not see any of the French Army. Our men called it "The Coffee Expedition," as we had no fighting.

While we stayed at this place we had orders to leave the country. The French army was coming down with such a large force, we were not able to meet them. We embarked at Cook's Haven the latter end of January, 1806; had a rough voyage. Our ship in Yarmouth Roads went down; a pilot came on board to conduct us into the harbour; in doing this he ran the ship on a sand-bank. She soon began to fill with water. It was a transport ship, the property of the captain; and not being copper bottomed, she soon went down; all was confusion on board. The captain swore he would hang the pilot at the yard-arm.

Signals were made to shore for boats to come out to our relief; and through mercy we were again preserved, and safely landed. The pilot managed to get into one of the first boats. We were quartered one night in Yarmouth. We never heard the result of the pilot's misfortune. We marched next morning to a place called Lowestoft, and we saw the masts of our own sunken vessel above water; we thought she might be got up when the tide was down. Thus, our first trip at sea was a perilous one, both in going to the continent, and also in returning to England.

Since I left the army my thoughts have often dwelt on that portion of the 107th Psalm:

> "They that go down to the sea in ships;
> that do business in great waters;
> these see the works of the Lord,
> and his wonders in the deep;
> for he commandeth and raiseth the stormy wind,
> which lifteth up the waves thereof,
> they mount up to the Heaven;
> they go down again to the depths;
> their soul is melted because of trouble;
> they reel to and fro and stagger like a drunken man,
> and are at their wit's end.
> Then they cry unto the Lord in their trouble,
> and he bringeth them out of their distress.
> He maketh the storm a calm,
> so that the waves thereof are still.
> Then are they glad because they be quiet;

so he bringeth them unto their desired haven."

Thus our lives in both cases we owe to his care:

Who the winds and the waters obey; -
Although, poor thoughtless wretches then most of us were;
Nor had we a heart then to pray!
To his mercy we owe both our safety and health,
When dangers encompassed us round,
Who gives us our comforts, provisions, and wealth,
Who now stands on free British ground!

We stayed at Lowestoft a few days, and were then marched to Woodbridge Barracks; and shortly afterwards to Colchester.

It was not my lot to stay in England long.

Chapter 2

On the 28th of April, 1806, the company I belonged to with two more, were ordered to march to Harwich, to embark on an expedition to Sweden, under the command of that brave hero Sir John Moore.

A Captain Grant, and Lieut. Leighton had something unpleasant between them at the Officers' mess. Capt. Grant was not going on the expedition, but Lieut. Leighton was. Capt. Grant followed us, overtook us, and was determined to fight a duel on the road — we did not hear it — we heard the pistol-shot fired, and Capt. Grant was killed on the spot! Lieut. Leighton was not allowed to go on the expedition. The case was tried at Chelmsford, and the lieutenant, was acquitted.

We sailed for Sweden, and anchored in Gottenburg harbour; six weeks we lay at anchor there, while Sir John Moore went to Stockholm to negotiate with the Swedish government. We were to assist the Swedes against the Russians, but Sir John returned to Gottenburg, and we came back to Colchester.

My next trip was to Copenhagen, July, 1807. A large fleet of line of battle and troop ships were fitted out for the Baltic; the land forces under the command of Lord Cathcart, and the naval forces under the command of Admiral Gambier. We again bid adieu to Old England, and had a pleasant voyage through the North Sea. The whole fleet anchored at Elsinore Castle, which mounted, I believe, more than 100 pieces of cannon. I never witnessed such a large and fine fleet as this before. The next morning we weighed anchor, and sailed up the sounds towards Copenhagen; signals were then made to disembark; the flat bottomed boats were manned with British troops, and the sailors had a cannon in each boat, and we all pushed off to the shores of Denmark, and landed without any opposition on the part of the enemy.

It was a beautiful sight to see so many boats manned with soldiers and sailors. As we were forming into ranks, a party of sailors were to do the same. A sea officer was drilling them, as well as he could; he said, "come up starboard," and "fall back larboard;" and then said "come up both ends and go back in the middle:" which made us laugh.

When we had marched a few miles and saw no enemy, we needed a guide to direct us to Copenhagen, as we were some fifteen or twenty miles from the city. A Dane, who was without his coat, going to fetch his cows, was pressed as one, by the Duke of Wellington; (he was at that time Sir Arthur Wellesley). The guide was given in charge to me and my comrade. The poor fellow was unwilling to go with us! Sir Arthur bid us draw our swords, and this, had the desired effect; but the poor fellow cried and talked, though we could not understand one word he uttered; this was on the 16th of August, 1807.

The guide was shortly set at liberty, and was glad to go for his cows without being paid for his trouble. We then came to a village, pulled off our knapsacks, and laid ourselves down in the street, the weather being warm. The artillery came up, and some dragoons; our regiment joined them, thus forming the advanced guard. We met a Dane on horseback, who asked us, in broken English, if we were going to Copenhagen?

We said: "Yes."

He then said, "You will not be able to get in there! There is too much cannon, and too many troops to oppose you."

We told him "We should try what British guns and valour could do."

We then marched up very near the suburbs of the city, and had a fine view of it, it appeared to be a splendid place, well fortified with cannon, and surrounded with water. They had furnaces on the ramparts to heat shot red hot. One part of the city faced the sea. The British fleet moved up towards this part, but there was "The Three Crown Battery" to pass before any execution could be expected. Then another plan was resorted to: and that was, to land the lower tier of big guns of the line of battle ships, and make batteries around that part of the city, by labour of the sailors and part of the army.

The Danes had most of their regular troops in Copenhagen. They had also a strong force of Militia up the country; and the division to which I belonged, was sent with some cavalry and artillery in pursuit of them.

We found them near to a place called "Keogh," encamped, about 14,000. They saluted us with a cannon ball, which struck the ground and rolled a good way; I saw it! Our Colonel's horse was well nigh broken by it.

The Rifles pushed on in extended order, as is always the case in action. The 79th and 92nd Highlanders made a brilliant charge with the bayonet, and they soon dispersed; our cannon played through the town, and we overtook them: they were shod with wooden shoes, except the officers, so that it was impossible for them to run fast. I believe they were all taken prisoners!

About 1,000 of them made their way to a farmhouse, where they fired a few shots at us; and my comrade was wounded in the arm, and had the butt of his rifle shattered by a ball. It was our afternoon's work to hunt them down and bring them in the marketplace. Several of them were mortally wounded. Our loss was very trifling.

We marched to a place called Rosskeel, to headquarters; and being on sentry one night about nine o'clock, our colonel came past me, and asked me if I saw a light in a direction he pointed to?

I said "Yes sir, I think it is the moon rising."

He said "No! it is Copenhagen on fire, if I am not mistaken."

He was right in his conjectures, for sure it was so. In two days after I was ordered out from headquarters, with a detachment of 12 men, a sargeant, a corporal, and a dragoon, to the King of Denmark's Palace, his country seat, and were furnished with three days' provisions when we arrived at the Palace.

The steward took all our store of provisions and gave it to the dogs; and although his Majesty was not there, we lived like kings on the fat of the land. Rum, wine, brandy, and the best eatables in Denmark, were profusely provided for us. The knives and forks, and spoons, were all of silver. We stayed there about 14 days; and then were called unto headquarters. We were conveyed there in spring waggons, at the steward's request.

By this time our troop had been called into Copenhagen to extinguish the fires our shells and rockets had made; and things were so settled that we were to have all their fleet, and gun boats, with all the arsenal stores which were in the harbour. When we marched through the place to go on ship-board, I was astonished to see the havoc our bombardment had made. Whole streets lay in ruins; churches burnt down; and we had hard work to get through the streets to the dock-yard, and to go on board, our road being blocked up with bricks, stones, tiles and timber.

I was put on board a line of battle-ship called the Agamemnon, 64 guns, commanded by Captain Ross; and never being on board a man-of-war before, I went down between decks; it appeared to me like another world, all bustle but everything in its proper place. This gallant ship was engaged at the battle of Trafalgar, when she had two of the enemy's ships playing on her during the whole time of the action; she had three port holes knocked in one! I felt a little proud to sail to England in her.

When all was ready for sailing, the anchors were got up, and the whole of the Danish fleet came out of harbour; a line of battle ships, frigates, and a great number of gun boats, a Danish prize ship to each English ship of war, each ship firing a grand salute of 21 guns as we passed Elsinore Castle; and I thought what a ruinous plight Denmark must be in, their crops destroyed, a great part having been eaten by the British Cavalry; their fine city burned, and the whole of their fine fleet gone, with all the stores in the arsenal! I was told that if they had consented to the wishes of the British Government, they would have been restored to them in as good condition as when given up.

This fine fleet was in danger of being captured by the French. The gunboats could not be steered through the North Sea, so a carpenter was sent from each ship to plug them, and they were sunk. The prize of our ship was named The Princess Caroline, a two-decker.

We had a good passage to England, with the loss of one man only, and he was a sailor, (a fine young fellow); the hands were ordered aloft to take in a reef, and while attending to this part of his work, he missed his foot-hold, and fell from the rigging into the sea! We were sailing about 12 knots an hour; it was a very dark night; the ship was brought to, and a boat launched out, and manned, but the poor fellow sunk to rise no more! The captain cried, and said "he was one of the best hands of his crew."

At length we arrived within sight of the white cliffs of Britain, and anchored off Margate for the night; sailed on towards Dover, put on board lighters, and when the tide served, we went into harbour at midnight. When we jumped on shore we could not get billets. The bugles sounded the assembly, and we marched off to Hythe Barracks, a distance of 12 miles. This was the place we had lain at before, and the inhabitants were glad to see us, especially the landlords and liquor merchants. And thus ended our ups and downs in Denmark and Germany. I could not help but feel grateful to our Preserver, and was almost even then, careless as I was, ready and willing to adopt the following sentiment of our poet:-

> "He that o'er rules the deep waters and seas,
> And whom the most boisterous winds must obey;
> Can preserve us in dangers, we own if He please;
> Can o'er rule them for good in the dark cloudy day!
> Though the mind may be dark, as the dark cloudy night,
> He can break down the hardest, most obstinate will;
> He can say in such seasons, "Now let there be light";
> And to boisterous consciences too, "Peace! be still!"

Our next route was to Colchester in Essex.

Chapter 3

An expedition was fitted out in April, 1808, to go to Portugal. We marched to Portsmouth; and then sailed from Spithead to Lisbon; but through stress of weather, we had to put into Vigo Bay, in the north of Spain. We then sailed for the Burling Islands, and landed near to a place called Vimiera, on the 28th of August.

The battle of Vimiera was fought on the 21st; we had to march over the battle field; a great number lay unburied both French and English and some Portuguese. An armistice had been concluded between the English Commander and General Junot, who commanded the French troops. We had no other engagement, and Junot withdrew his troops into the city of Lisbon; and the British troops encamped on the heights of Bellam, about a mile from Lisbon.

In a few days it was so settled that the French were to go on board our shipping to France; so they marched down to the harbour with bands playing, colours flying, and bayonets fixed, with all the honours of war; and these same troops formed part of Marshal Soult's army that followed us to Corunna.

When the French had sailed, we went on board boats, and sailed over the river Tagus, where old Lisbon once stood, that had been destroyed by an earthquake. There are some of the old relics of it to be seen above water.

General Sir John Moore had the command of the British army, and a better officer never drew a sword; and whose loss was never more deeply felt by England as a nation.

We then marched into Spain, to Salamanca. The whole of the British army were about 25,000; we lay in convents. It was a splendid city, containing many thousands of inhabitants, with large shops; wine and every other commodity, very cheap. After lying here about two months, we marched further into Spain, and were quartered in the villages.

On one moonlight night we were ordered under arms, and

marched about seven or eight miles, when we were met by a Spanish guide, and orders were given to return to our respective cantonments. The cause of this was, we were told that 50,000 Spanish troops had laid down their arms, commanded by General Blake, an Irish gentleman. We saw them cowardly dispersing themselves, going over the mountains in droves. And this sad disaster was the cause of Sir John Moore's retreat to Corunna. So commenced this ever-memorable retreat on the 23rd of December, 1808, into the north of Spain.

A great deal of snow had fallen; and it fell to our lot, the light division, composed of the 43rd and 52nd light infantry, and the rifles, with the 7th, 10th, 15th, 18th, and a regiment of German hussars, to cover the retreat of the whole British army. Marshal Soult lost no time, with a very strong force of cavalry, infantry, and artillery, in driving us. Sir John Moore had received a very small reinforcement from England, under the command of Sir David Baird, who landed at Corunna. They had joined us but a short period when our retreat commenced; and in two or three days the French cavalry, forming their advanced guard, were close up to our rear, and teasing us from morning till night.

Their cavalry had a rifleman mounted behind each dragoon; and when any good position or bushes by the road side, gave them any advantage to give our men a few shots, those riflemen would dismount, and get under cover of the bushes: so that we were obliged to do the same; their dragoons at the same time dismounting, and laying their carbines on their saddles, with their horse standing in front of them for a sort of defence, would give us a few shots as well. In this way we were often obliged to make a stand and drive them back.

We had used to laugh to see the riflemen run to the road, put their feet into the stirrups, and mount behind the dragoons, and gallop back. We served many of these fellows off; and then we had to run to get up to the regiment. This was the sport for many days; and we could not avoid it.

It was a long march, about 250 miles, before we could arrive at Corunna. We had no tents; a blanket had been served out to each man; we marched from daylight until dark; the bullocks were driven before us; and slaughtered as they were needed; they had little or no fat on them. But if we had time to boil our mess well, we counted more of the soup than the meat, as it was so tough. But it was not often that we could do this, as we had no shelter but the canopy of heaven; and we seldom halted more than two hours; and having wood and water to seek to cook our victuals, before we could do so, the order would be given to get under arms and get on the march.

We had some artillery with us, six pounders; and we had to muffle the gun-wheels with grass, or anything we could find, to prevent the enemy from hearing us move; and we made up large fires, and moved on the road as still as possible. This was the game we had to play many nights; as the French advanced guard would seldom be more than half a mile from us, when we halted.

Our captains were all mounted, but the lieutenants had to walk, and I have seen some of them move on fast asleep until they have jostled on some of the men, and been thus awakened. They were long nights in the months of December and January.

At daylight the enemy would be close on our rear; they had seen our fires burn out; and then the day proved as the day before -- a continual harassing.

Many days we had no commissary with bread; our spirits so low with hunger and fatigue, that we often said we would as soon die as live!

We had several rivers to cross, and a large stone bridge across each; and when we came to these bridges, an engineer officer with three or four of his men, who had put a bag or barrel of powder under the main arch, and laid a long trail of loose powder some 40 or 50 yards, would ask "if all was over?" If the answer was "yes," they would put the slow match to the powder, and when it reached the cask or bag, the large arch would be blown into the air with a report as loud as thunder. Then he would say, "Now Mr Frenchman, you will be kind enough to halt, until we get on a mile or two." They carried on mules temporary bridges, or planks, and they were quick in laying them down, and their troops were soon in sight; and we would as soon have them in sight, as out of it; as it rested our weary limbs to lie down, and give them a few rifle balls; as lying down, or kneeling to fire was our general mode in action.

The roads being very bad, the British army could not move on very fast, I think not more than two miles an hour. Our colonel had orders for us to throw away our knapsacks, but keep either the great coat, or blanket, which we chose. We did not mind parting with our kits, our orders must be obeyed, so we left them by the road side. But we then had enough to carry; fifty round of ball cartridge; thirty loose balls in our waist belt; and a flask, and a horn of powder; and rifle, and sword; the two weighing 14 pounds. These were plenty for us to carry; with empty bellies, and the enemy close at our heels, thirsting for our blood!

Many of our men sat down by the road-side, and gave up the ghost, fairly worn down! Those who could use tobacco held out the best. I was one of this number. We had seven or eight women belonging to the regiment. There were no baggage wagons on which they could ride; and some of them fell into the hands of the enemy; and after using them as they pleased, they gave them some food, and sent them to us!

When we had marched two or three hours on a night, our colonel would give the word to halt, for the purpose that the men might do what they wanted; and I have seen many who did not want to fall out of the ranks for that purpose, drop down nine or ten on each other, some with big coats on, some with blankets; and they would be fast asleep on the snow, huddled together, in the space of a minute; and when the word was given to "fall in," the sergeants would have to kick them very hard to awaken them.

One moon light night I saw one of our men walk into a pit of water; he had got off the road but the water soon made him open his eyes! I have proved, on this retreat that a man will wear down a horse, I have seen 30 or 40 of the horses of the hussar regiment knock up in a day. When they were taken lame, and could not keep up with the troops the rider was ordered to dismount; throw his saddle bags on his shoulder, draw his pistol, and fire the ball through his horse's head; leaving him, with the saddle and all the other trappings, and the poor fellows would have to walk with knee boots and spurs, in the best manner they could to Corunna. We felt sorry for them, as they were not used to walking.

Chapter 4

We arrived one morning at a large town called Lugo; but before we entered the place, some of the foot guards were cooking; their belts hanging on the bushes.

It appeared that Sir John Moore had halted the army at this place, with a view to give Marshal Soult battle. Some of the guards asked us if we had seen the French? Our answer was "yes!" and "so will you soon! you had better get your belts on, and be ready, and lay by cooking!" They would not believe the enemy was so near; but before we were settled in the town we heard plenty of shots fired; and the guards would both see, and feel them, ere we were quartered on the inhabitants; we had twenty-four hours' rest, and our sleep was sweet unto us, and we got our rations; both meat, bread, and wine.

Our army had a good position; but Soult did not come to a general action! The next morning our brave troops got on the march; it was fourteen leagues from Lugo to Corunna, English measure; and our light division had to form the rearguard. Leaving this place we saw a great many pieces of Spanish cannon; but no artillery to man them. These guns were all spiked; so that they could be of no use to the enemy!

One of our men an habitual drunkard, could not march; he was so full of red port! So our colonel bid the bugle-major cut all the buttons off his jacket, that the French might not know what an honourable regiment he belonged to.

Whether he was killed or taken prisoner, we never knew! A prisoner to old Alcohol he was; and a prisoner to the French he might be! He had seen better days; his name was Thomas Baxter; he was an excellent scholar; had been an attorney, and at one period rode in his carriage; he was made corporal, and sergeant, many times; but he always got reduced and disgraced, through drunkenness! So much for Alcohol's prisoner!

We marched off next, to a place called Bellefranco, and it nighted when we arrived there, the English stores were set on fire to prevent them falling into the hands of the French! We thought the town was on fire, but it proved only to be the stores and some baggage.

The next place was a large town called Estergan, and here the 2nd batalion took the road for Vigo, a seaport in Spain, with some other regiments; this weakened our force, but Soult's army did not follow them. We next came to a town called Kankabella, and a short distance before we reached the place, we saw three regiments formed in a square. Sir John Moore was present. We were ordered to join these troops. A soldier had been tried by court martial, and was sentenced to be hanged. He had the rope round his neck, fastened to the branch of a tree and sat upon two men's shoulders, with a cap drawn over his face, waiting the signal for the two men to let him drop, when Sir John Moore, with a loud voice, said:

"If I forgive this man, will the army be answerable for his future good conduct?"

Our brave colonel said "yes?" and the word "yes" went through the ranks three times, and the man's life was spared! I never knew what regiment he belonged to!

When this scene was over, our calvary came in at full gallop, and the French close at their heels. Sir John, with his staff, were near being made prisoners. They bid us get into the houses and fire out of the windows. Many of our men did; but they were taken prisoners.

We got through the town, and made a stand on the bridge. A large river ran by the town, and on this bridge brave Captain Dickenson was killed, and several other men were killed, or wounded. Some of our men swam through the river. One of the 7th hussars had got dismounted from his horse, and was near the French cavalry; he said:

"I will fetch my horse if I am killed in the attempt."

We told him he had better not try, but he ran over the bridge, and mounted his horse; the French fired several shots at him, but all missed both him and his horse!

We then extended in chain order; it was getting dark; we had missed the main road, and were in some grape vines. I fell into a well, but there was no water in it, and two more men fell in; one called out for help, when some of our comrades come and pulled us out. The well was I think about five or six feet deep.

Here I had the misfortune to lose my hat, cap, and forage cap, and the lock cap of my rifle, and my sword was broke in the scabbard by the fall. When I was pulled out I was greatly stunned by the accident, and the two other men falling on me, I thought my thigh was broke. I lay down a few moments, and then tried to walk.

At a short distance to our left, we heard some men speaking English, but could not see them; they said, "here is the main road," so we closed to our left, and joined them.

The party proved to be our out-laying picquet, so we halted a few minutes, that we might all close; and an officer of ours had the command of this party. We soon heard the sound of horses' feet in our rear; our officer said: "It is the English cavalry," but in a moment the word "Qui vive," (in English "who comes there,") convinced us that they were the French advance guard. They fired their pistols on our men, but I was so lame I fell down on the grass by the road side. They rode past me, and my clothing being green, they did not see me.

Our men gave them a few shots; they wheeled to the "right about;" and when they were riding by me, I began to think "my doom is a French prison," but they did not then see me. When they passed me a short distance, I rose up, but it was some time before I could overtake my party.

> "My cap was gone, my head was bare;
> Twas a cold dark night I do declare!
> My sword likewise was broke in two;
> And O, I thought, "what must I do?"

I told my misfortune to the captain, and all he said to me about it, was "It is a good thing you didn't break your neck;"

I was able to keep up with the party, as our marching was slow. In a short time the moon rose, and we overtook some general's baggage. I saw a glazed hat tied on one of the mules; I asked my comrade to lend me his knife, when I cut the string and put the hat on; but it was so large it came over my eyes; I padded it with some grass, and it did very well.

About the middle of the night we halted, and turned into a chapel; some hussars were in, and also their horses. We were so jammed and crushed that we could not all lie down. We got on the march before daylight, and passed a cart drawn by a yoke of oxen, which was laden with English stores and some boots and shoes. The oxen were knocked up; they could get no further; so the cargo was distributed amongst us. I got a pair of boots, put them on, and threw my old ones away; but before I had walked four miles the bottom of one boot dropped off, the upper leather remaining laced round my ankle. Going three or four miles further the other boot bottom dropped off, and I had to walk barefoot, as my stocking feet were soon cut all to pieces. I was not alone in this predicament; many of the men were served the same.

These boots were manufactured in England, and we said the soles and heels had been glued or pegged on, as there could not have been any wax or hemp used, and the person who contracted with the government ought to have been tried by court-martial, and to have been rewarded with a good flogging with a cat-o'-nine-tails; and I for one should like to have given them 200 lashes each for their tricking tricks!

Next morning some of our officers were offering the men a guinea for a pair of boots or shoes, as the baggage goods were all thrown away, and they were in as bad a plight as the privates.. I felt sorry to see gentlemen of good fortune and talent exposed to such privations, as no doubt they would think of their good homes, left to encounter the fatigues of war, and to be involved in one of the most disastrous retreats that ever British troops were led to experience; but:

Talent, and money, and influence here,
Are all of them nothing in such scenes as these;
Though the great, and the wealthy, might feel very queer,
Yet they are subject to trials like us, 'cross the seas!
Blister'd feet, worn but stockings, and boots without soles
Are the portion of many, who go out to war;

Where the wide swelling billows o'er each other rolls,
There are troubles for soldiers and each jolly tar!
We may think of their woes when we sit by our fire;
We may mourn o'er the fate of e'en thousands at sea,
Who fall 'neath the stroke of some cannon-ball dire;
But we'll pray "From all evils like these keep us free!"

Chapter 5

We had arrived within four leagues of Corunna, and my company being on outlaying picquet, we were surprised when daylight began to appear, to see a red-coated soldier, and a woman in our rear. We asked the man how it was he was behind his regiment? He belonged to the 91st Scotch.

He told us his wife had been taken in labour about 12 o'clock the over night in an out-house, or hovel, and the doctor of the regiment had attended her. She had been delivered of a fine child. The doctor told the man to stay with his wife, and submit to be taken by the enemy. This the soldier agreed to do; but in the morning before daylight appeared, she said to him:

"I don't like the thoughts of your going to a French prison; and I don't know how ill the French may use me; I will try to get up and walk."

She had no shoes or stockings, and the babe was wrapped in an apron, or shawl. She was almost famished. On the over night we had been served out with three days bread and pork. We gave her some. She had tasted nothing all the day before. We told them to make the best of their way. Whether the poor woman reached Corunna, or died on the road, it is not for me to say. I have often thought of her, and talked to others about the affecting scene.

They had not left us above half an hour, before we had orders not to move until broad daylight appeared; when the advanced guard of the French came in sight at full trot, so we retreated, then joined the regiment. The engineer officer was waiting our arrival. A bridge was to be blown up as soon as we were over.

After the explosion one of our men fixed himself behind a large stone, under cover from the enemy, and fired fourteen balls; he killed or wounded at every shot. He bid us bring him more ammunition, as he had fired off every round he had. He was so near the enemy that no one dared to take him any, so he ran to us. Several shots were fired at him, but all missed!

We advanced towards Corunna, and left the French to repair the bridge we had blown up. On the 12th of January 1809, we came in sight of the city. The enemy not making their appearance, we made fires and cooked our meat, took off our belts, sponged out our rifles, got a fresh supply of ammunition, took off our jackets, and found plenty of vermin on our bodies, which in some cases had found their way into flesh, as well as appearing outside. As knapsacks, and razors, and kitt, were all thrown away, some of the older men had beards like Jews; not having been shaved since the commencement of the retreat.

And now another disaster arose to add to all our suffering in hunger, cold, and the long march of 250 miles. The shipping could not get round from Vigo Bay to take us on board; the wind not being fair. Steamers in 1809 we had none.

Marshall Soult was increasing his forces on the 14th and 15th, so that on the morning of the 16th it was reported that he had about 70,000 effective troops. Our number was under 20,000.

On the 14th, in the morning, Sir John Moore gave orders for our great magazines, containing some tons of powder, and balls to be blown up, as it could not be shipped. We were about a mile distant when the explosion took place. It shook the earth where we stood!

On the 15th the 52nd regiment was an outlaying picquet. The French had sent out, in front of their army, a number of sharp-shooters to attack our position. The 52nd were driven in. The bugle sounded the advance, and double-quick for the rifles, to attack their sharp-shooters.

I had been attacked for a few days with the bloody flux; and was often obliged to wait on myself, my comrades had retreated; and having to sit down, I was the only mark the French had to fire at. Several balls struck the ground near me, but they all missed, and I escaped unhurt; but I was so jaded that I would quite as soon be killed as not!

On the 15th we received orders to be ready to embark. The wind had shifted a few points, so that the vessels had worked round from Vigo Bay, to Corunna harbour; and we were pleased with this good news; but alas! we were not to get on board until a vast deal more blood must be spilt!

Marshal Soult was anxious for a general engagement. We passed the afternoon pretty quiet; yet a little skirmishing between the armies was carried on. We made our fires at night; the French did the same; we lay down with our great coats on; and near me lay our brave Colonel Beckwith, and our Adjutant Stewart; they both wrapped themselves up in their boat cloaks; and some of the men feathered some straw, and covered them from the cold. At daylight, on the 16th (Sunday), the Adjutant rose from his bed, and rubbing the straw off his trousers, saw, and caught a large louse.

"And are you surprised at finding one, Mr Stewart?" said the colonel.

He replied "I am."

The colonel answered "I have plenty about me; and I'll engage there is not a man in the whole army that is wholly free! How can it be otherwise, when knapsacks and baggage are all thrown away?" The colonel rose, put his spy-glass to his eye, looked towards the French camp, and said "Though we are under orders for embarkation, mark my word for it, we shall have something to do in another shape; for I see Soult is preparing for an attack!"

And so it turned out; for as we were attending with our camp kettles for our daily wine, a cannon ball was fired at us from the French. Our bugles sounded the advance; away went the kettles; the word was given "Rifles in front extended by files in chain order!" The enemy's sharp shooters were double and triple our numbers. We soon got within range of their rifles, and began to pick them off. We held them in check till our light division formed in line, and then the carnage commenced.

The roar of cannon and the roll of musketry was so loud, that without great attention the word of command could scarcely be given, and the sound of the bugle hardly heard. If a bystander, out of reach of shot or shell, could have seen the two armies, they would have concluded our small force of about 14,000, against between 60,000 or 70,000, must have been all cut off. British valour, skill, and courage, was to be tested.

We were well supplied with powder and ball, all fresh and good.

We fought more desperate, as the enemy had deprived us of our daily allowance of wine. There were many enclosures of stone walls, and these walls gave our sharpshooters a good cover. We made what are called loop-holes to fire through. We spent a great deal of ball cartridge.

I saw Sir John Moore riding along our line at full gallop with his staff. About half an hour after we heard he was wounded. We fought from two o'clock till six. It then became dark and the firing almost ceased.

Our noble commander was carried into Corunna in a blanket by four grenadiers of the 20th regiment, and General Hope took the command. We had an officer killed of my company whose name was Noble; his brother-in-law was Major Northcott. He offered two dollars (9/-) to any man who would bring his watch, sword, and sash, and cover his body with stones. He was shot dead close to a stone wall; but it was so dark that they could not find him; the Major cried; he had married Lieut. Noble's sister. Our loss in the regiment was not so great as might have been expected, after four hours' fighting. We then made our fires for the night; and remained on the battlefield until five o'clock in the morning, when an order came for us to move on into Corunna.

Ours was the last regiment that left the battle-field. The French seeing our fires getting low, were soon on the alert. In passing over the drawbridge into the city, the 23rd regiment had the charge of us. We marched through the streets into the harbour; the boats of the men of war, and transport ships pushed to the shore to take us on board; but what confusion was there! Many of the hussars' horses were galloping on the beach like mad things. There was not time to embark them. Several were shot or we should have been rode over, or trodden to death.

By this time Soult had got six pieces of cannon playing on the ships and boats. The vessels were at anchor. We got into any ship or boat we could. The sailors from the shore rowed to the ship. The grape shot from the French guns came plentifully through the rigging of the ships, as well as amongst the soldiers of the boat. But presently an English line of battleship weighed her anchor and sailed within range of the French guns, and crippled four of them out of the six. I think the ship was called the Bellorophon. A signal was then made for the master transports to cut their cables, leave the anchors aground, and get out of harbour to see poor old England!

> What thinking man can view the scenes
> Just now recorded here,
> Or younger persons in their teens,
> And not let fall a tear!
> O when will war and bloodshed cease,
> O when will mortals learn
> To live in love, and cherish peace,
> And fiend-like battles spurn!
> The doctrines of the Prince of Peace,
> Back'd by the spirit's power,
> Alone can cause such strife to cease,
> And to learn "war no more!"
> O hasten, Lord, the happy day,
> Spread thine own truth around,
> And grant that every nation may
> List to the joyful sound!
> Thy word of everlasting Truth
> We know thou canst fulfil;
> Then grant that aged men, and youth,
> May learn and do Thy will!

General Hill's division remained until next day, to bring off the wounded. We were mustered the next morning to know what rations to draw. Our force was 61 men, rank and file, and one sergeant. We belonged to 29 different regiments. We had no officer on board. A sergeant of ours had the command. We had also twelve horses belonging to the staff. We had a rough passage of 18 days.

Chapter 6

On the 3rd of February we arrived at Spithead, and on the 4th we marched to Hilsey Barracks, three miles from Portsmouth. Such a lot of rag-a-muffins never landed at Portsmouth before. We were so filthy with vermin, we were not fit to sleep in any decent bed. Our route was to Hythe Barracks, in Kent. This was the headquarters for the Rifle Brigade. Our new clothing was served out, and then a fire was made in the barrack square, and all our clothing, shirts, and flannels we burned, and all the live stock they contained!

We did not know our loss in killed, wounded and missing, for several days after we arrived, as some landed at different ports, and some were wrecked off Plymouth. I think it was about three weeks before we all assembled, and when the paymaster had mustered the rest, our ranks had been thinned to a great amount.

An order was then issued from the war office for the Militia to volunteer; we had a good share of them. Our 1st and 2nd battalions we filled up to 1,000 each; and the 3rd battalion raised 1,000.

We expected that we were to have a long respite from war; but it did not prove so, for the men who had joined us from the militia had scarcely learned the rifle drill before the route came for the 1st battalion to embark at Dover.

We had received two guineas per man for loss of our kits. Our knapsacks had not come from London; but we got them when we arrived at Spithead.

On the 24th of May, 1809, we went on board at Dover; it was such a parting scene that I never wish to witness again. The women clung round the necks of their husbands, so that the officers had much ado to part them. There was such ringing of hands, tearing of hair, and crying, that I was glad to jump into the boat; and I felt thankful that I had no wife to bewail my loss! A great many very respectable inhabitants of Dover stood around to witness our departure; and amongst the females many tears were shed, while they looked on to see a thousand fine young fellows push off in the boats from the harbour to the ships, which lay at anchor about a mile from the shore. Three cheers were given from the shore, which were responded to by us in the boats.

The next morning we sailed onward to Spithead, when we received our knapsacks, as before hinted, from London. Here the 43rd and 52nd regiments were on board, light infantry, waiting our arrival. We were glad to see them, and they cheered us. These two regiments composed the light division, with ours, in Sir John Moore's retreat.

On Sunday afternoon, about 4 o'clock, the signal was given from the commodore to weigh anchor. The wind being fair, we had a fair passage, and the whole fleet dropped anchor in the river Tagus, in front of Lisbon, on Thursday afternoon. I believe the distance is 900 miles. Thus we were near to the enemy's shore, in about four days. We soon landed, collected our force together in Black Horse Square.

Our line of march was through Portugal into Spain; and Lord Wellington being up in that part with the British army, had orders to join him as soon as we could; and to accomplish this we had some days double stages. It was very hot, in the month of July; we made the open fields our beds, and our knapsacks our pillows, having no tents on this long march. Two of our men dropped from the heat of the sun, and died! At length we arrived within 18 or 20 miles of Talavera, and heard the roaring of the cannon.

The next day we came to a place called Orapeasor. Several Spanish soldiers also came there, who were wounded in the battle. We marched the whole of the night, with the exception of two hours' halting to rest our weary limbs and cook our days' meat.

About 6 o'clock on the morning of the 29th we arrived on the battle-field. Lord Wellington came a mile or more to meet us. The battle ended on the 28th. We walked over the dead and wounded of both armies; and such a sight I never witnessed before!

A solemn awe seemed to pervade every breast to hear the groans of the wounded; the poor fellows begging for water, and to be carried out of the field into the town for shelter from the heat of the sun; but we were not permitted to do these acts of kindness, for our orders were to take the advance post amongst some olive trees near the river, on the other side of it, from the place of battle! The French artillery were all formed in parks; the infantry and cavalry covering their guns.

The scene after this battle had a great effect on some of the men who joined us from the militia. A young lad in my company from the "East Devon," was so sickened that he went to the hospital, and died! On our advance we came to some huts that our troops had made for shelter, and here lay some poor fellows of the 31st regiment, or, as they are called, "the Young Buffs," bayoneted in their huts where they lay! It appeared the enemy had come upon them in the night; I should expect after the day's action, as the palms of their hands, and their faces were covered with live magots!

I unbuttoned one man's knapsack, hoping to find a shirt, as I stood in great need of one. The poor fellow had some well written letters about him, from his wife in Ireland. I perused one of them; it appeared he had three children. I kept the letter; and a short time after an order was issued through the camp, for the letters to England to be ready on the next day. I felt it my duty to answer the poor woman's letter, to let her know the fate of her husband, and did so.

We remained at this camp eight or nine days. The smell of the dead was awful. Fatigue parties were burning them, the weather was so hot! At length a general order was given to cut branches from the trees, cover the bodies with them and burn them.

The French had retreated, and we soon after had to move, as the fever had seized many of our men.

We could not buy anything to eat, and our rations were scant. We had been used to a pint of red port served to every man daily; but here none could be had, "neither for love nor money." It is true we could get meat every day, as the bullocks were driven before us, and slaughtered as they were needed. But the staff of life was broken; bread and wine, the two principal things to sustain a soldier on a long march! As we had no tents, we took the fields and weather, as it pleased the Lord to send it. Officers and men fared alike! We have been six or seven days without tasting bread.

We sometimes encamped under acorn trees after a long day's

march. A certain number of men would be appointed to each tree to pluck the acorns, which are much larger than those that grow here. We boiled them in the camp kettles, and when the husks were peeled off they ate something like a potato. Once, after a long day's march, we halted near a corn field; the general of the division rode up to our colonel, and said, "the men had better carry some of the wheat, as there is no prospect of any provisions."

We carried sheaves of it on our rifles, and when we halted for the night, we set to work to cook it; and first we cut the heads of the wheat off, and put them into our haversacks, and thrashed with the ramrod, then winnowed it with our breath; "then go and look out for a spring of water, if happily one was near!" But we often hunted for it and returned without any. Thus in our extremity, and with difficulty, we at length boiled some, and had to eat it without salt, for none could be bought! The next morning, however, many were so swelled that they could not march that day.

We next came to what we called the "Stony Camp." We had to clear the stones away before we could lay ourselves down to rest; and here we had to hunt after a young stirk, or a large calf; and some of the men kept up the chase for about an hour. At length the poor thing was run down, and I believe life was not extinct before some of the meat was broiling on the fire, or boiling in the camp kettles. Those who ran the poor beast down did not allow time to take off the skin, it was hacked up with swords and bill-hooks, and soon eaten! I never saw such a barbarous act before, and could not help feeling thankful that I had no part in it.

> That a Soldier's life's not very easy,
> From these statements our friends may all see;
> Though some may be call'd "fat and lazy,"
> At that time 'twas not so with me!
> Though our enemies from us retreated,
> We found quite enough to endure,
> As the facts we so freely have stated,
> Will convince our kind friends we are sure
> Though our swords were put up for a season,
> Except to cut up the poor calf,

They may see we had little reason
To banish our woes with a laugh!
Our foes we well know might come on us,
Even when we were all fast asleep,
And those who were "hardly torn from us,"
Might then vent their sorrows and weep!

On our march we ascended some high hills, where we made what is called a grand stand! Marshal Soult was in full pursuit of us. The river being between us and the French, their cavalry thought they would give us a few shots; but we did not heed them; and as the river was not fordable, we bid them defiance.

It was hunger we were experiencing, and gave us the most uneasiness. In this encampment we had four ounces of flour per man served out, which we mixed with water, made it up into small balls, and boiled them. As they were less than dumplings, we called them dough-boys, and hence we called this encampment "Dough-boy Hill!"

A town's-lad of mine came to me one Sunday and said:

"Bill, I think we shall be kept on this Dough-boy Hill till we shall all die of want."

I said, "I think so too;" and added, "It is Lutterworth feast today; our friends will be eating the plum pudding and roast beef!"

"Ah!" said he, "they little think what we pass through and suffer."

I said, "Cheer up, lad, we shall see better days yet!"

I saw him but once after that day; he was then sick from fever, and riding on a mule; but he soon died, as did many more.

Chapter 7

O how uncertain are all things here. We stayed on our own named "Dough-boy Hill" nine or ten days. By the time we arrived in Portugal we had about 5000 sick in Elvas Hospital, and the greater part died there.

This town is a very large place, well fortified, with a strong and high wall 30 or 35 feet high, mounted with cannon. It is a frontier garrison, about 12 miles from Badajos.

The light division to which I belonged was stationed at a place called "Campo-Mayo." This was a walled-in-town, but no cannon to ward off an enemy.

There we stayed five or six weeks. The hospital was soon filled with sick; the fever was so raging that many went in on the morning and at night were carried out to the grave-yard. Our doctor used a very singular expedient, which was this: we were ordered when off duty to sit up with the sick in our turns, and about midnight to take each one out of bed, as they all lay without shirts, and lead them to a flight of steps, and pour two buckets of cold water on each; they were so deranged they knew nothing about it. I have put my finger into their hand, when they would jump out of bed, follow me, and sit quietly while we poured the contents of the buckets over them, and would be led by the finger back again to bed, and never utter one word; and it was thought by the officers and doctors, that this mode of treatment had a good effect.

Those who died were buried without shells about eleven or twelve o'clock at night, without any burial service, and without firing over them! A young man in the same company as myself, a native of Hinckley, fell ill of the fever, was taken to the dead-house, laid on a plank, with his feet tied together; he was to have been buried the same night. As the sentinel was on his post he heard a noise in the dead-house; he called the corporal of the guard, the door was opened, and the poor fellow had fell off the plank, and was trying to get the string off his feet. He got well and joined in the ranks with me after that. His name was John Moore.

While we remained at this place, a man of the 88th regiment attempted to desert to the French. He was taken to headquarters at Badajos, and tried by court-martial, found guilty, and sentenced to death! I saw him executed. He deserved his fate! A man that takes the Queen's bounty, and runs over to the enemy's camp, might give the enemy much information as to the strength and position of our armies, and cause the death of many of his comrades; therefore, in my opinion, ought to suffer as a traitor. So this man's blood fell on his own head.

At this place a German of the 60th regiment, a Frenchman, and two Italians, belonging the "Chasseurs Britannica," were shot for desertion. On the morning that the sentence of the first was carried into execution, the division was assembled outside the town, where they formed three sides of a square. The prisoner was marched past the various regiments by the chaplain of the division, and the guard appointed to shoot him.

When his devotions were finished, he was blindfolded by the Provost Marshal, and placed in a kneeling position on the brink of his grave; he gave the signal, and the next moment he fell into it, pierced with half-a-dozen musket balls. The different regiments then passed the body, with the words, "eyes left", as they passed him.

The evening previous to the others being shot, the Serjeant came with the company's books to settle their accounts. The two Italians were in great agony, wringing their hands. The Frenchman who had been taken prisoner, and had volunteered into the "Chasseurs Britannica," and afterwards deserted, in his behaviour, formed a strong contrast to the others. Calm and dignified, he seemed to feel no fear of death, nor did any complaint pass his lips, save the injustice of trying him as a deserter; he said:

"Being a Frenchman, it was natural that he should join his friends the first opportunity that offered!"

When the serjeant was settling their accounts, every item was noticed with the greatest exactness, and the serjeant wanting a small coin, about the value of a farthing, to balance, he desired him to produce it before he would sign the ledger! But though thus exact with the sergeant, the moment he received his balance, which amounted to some dollars, he divided every penny of it among his fellow prisoners!

He continued to walk about with his arms folded the whole evening, without seeming the least disturbed. It was reported he was a brother of Marshal Soult; but the truth of which I cannot pretend to affirm. He was a man of noble mind and independent spirit; elegant in person, and handsome in features. About midnight he lay down and slept soundly until the time of execution. He cleaned himself with the greatest nicety. The guard having arrived, he took leave of his fellow prisoners, and said:

"Remember, I die a Frenchman!"

He marched off to the place of execution with the same courage; and when he was shot all were sorry for him.

From this place (Campo-Mayo) we retreated further into Portugal, as Marshal Soult was advancing with a strong army; and Lord Wellington gave up Badajos to the Spanish troops. Soult was determined to take it if possible.

Lord Wellington had told the Spanish governor to hold out, and he would send him supplies; but he acted in the most cowardly manner, and gave up that stronghold into the hands of the French! And this was a bad blow for the British and Portuguese army; it caused us a great deal of marching and countermarching for a long time, when we might have been quiet in our camps in the summer, and snug in our cantonments in the winter!

We never put much confidence in the Spanish troops, they too often acted a cowardly part. We used to call them "bad-plucked ones;" they would rather run than fight! Not so the Portuguese, they fought well, they were mixed with the British and fought like men! They were hardy good soldiers; and proved it by their conduct in the field.

This Peninsular war was a continual harassing, we never had rest or ease long together. If in the winter we were in our cantonments we could not take off our clothes; and when off duty, and retired in the houses, we were allowed to take off our stocks and jackets only; to be ready at a few minutes' notice, or to turn out at the first sound of the bugle. Our practice was often to get under arms an hour before daylight; and to stand under arms until broad day, when the enemy were near. The French did the same.

> What a noble example is this, friends for us!
> For us who are rallying round Jesus' cross!
> In the Frenchman we learn to be true to our cause,
> To be true to our country, our bible, our laws!
> In the Soldiers who rose up a while before day,
> We may see its our duty those laws to obey!
> So that when the last bugle or trumpet may sound
> 'Mongst our great Captain's soldiers we all may be found.

Chapter 8

We were lying near a village called "Barbi de Poque," in three companies, and near this village was a river with a bridge across between two hills.

The French had a strong picquet on the other side of this river. There was a winding zig-zag narrow path down to this bridge, some 200 yards from the top of the hill. At night we placed a double sentinel at the foot of the bridge and the French did the same. At day-light the double sentinels were withdrawn; a corporal and six men were posted in the night about half way down the hill, and a sergeant and 12 men on the top. A Roman Catholic chapel, some 300 yards distant, we had for a picquet house.

The French and us were so near that we could speak to each other. In the day time we had orders not to fire unless they came over the bridge. We used to hold up our canteens of wine and ask them to come over and drink with us. They would answer in the Spanish language, "They would come that night." We little thought they would make the attempt but they did.

I was on sentry at our colonel and adjutant's lodgings that night. I was put on my post at 9 a.m. and was to be relieved at 11 o'clock p.m. The adjutant came out and asked me the time of night?

I said, "It is about 10, sir."

He said, "The colonel and me sleep in this lower room; if any alarm is made you will tap at this window."

When I was relieved I gave this additional order to the man who took my post. I went to the picquet-house, put my rifle in a certain place, lay down with the men, and dropped asleep; it was still and quiet. About 12 o'clock I was awoke by the voice of the officers with the words "Be quick men, and load as you go to the brow of the hill!" I jumped up, got my rifle, and overtook them.

I heard the firing; the double sentinels at the bridge were made prisoners; the corporal and six men were driven up to the sergeant, and the 12 at the brow of the hill. About 500 big grenadiers, half drunk, had made a rush over, and extending themselves, were climbing the rocks, and out-flanked our little company, both right and left. We challenged them, they answered our little company, both right and left.

We challenged them, they answered "We are Spaniards."

Our officer said "Don't fire, men, they are not French."

The words were scarcely out of his mouth, when a musket-ball struck him on the head, and he was a corpse in a minute.

The moon shone very bright, so that we could see them; they were spent out climbing up the rocks. Three of these big ugly fellows came within ten yards of me and my front-rank man; I had got my ball in my rifle, but had not time to return the ramrod, so both ball and ramrod went through one of them. My comrade fired, and the ball struck another in the breast. I threw my rifle down, as it was no use to me without a ramrod, and retired about 20 yards. A sergeant of ours lay on his back, a musket ball having passed through his belly.

I said "Sergeant Bradley, are you wounded?" He was groaning, poor fellow; and I said "Lend me your rifle I have fired my ramrod away with the ball! I had not time to return it, as the Frenchman had his firelock at his shoulder, and probably in another moment I might have been killed or wounded!" The sergeant bid me take his rifle, and said:

"It is of no use to me, they have done me, I am dying!"

I left him; and running to join my comrade, I saw our officer stretched on his back, his sword in one hand, and his spy-glass in the other.

I said "Mr Mercer, are you wounded?" but his spirit had fled.

By this time our other two companies had come from the village to our assistance, the colonel and adjutant with them. The colonel was a tall man about six feet one inch high; he had had a ball through his cap, but was not wounded; he soon rallied the enemy down the hill, and as they retreated to the bridge, they dragged their wounded with them. We took about 50 prisoners, and killed about 60 men.

We were then posted in chain order, and remained so until daylight.

The enemy had paid dear for their attack on us in the night, and when the morning appeared, we found they had retreated. We were ordered to climb the rocks to see if there were any wounded. Me and my comrade found a young Frenchman with his head in the hole of a rock, and his legs and part of his body were visible.

I said "Here's a wounded Frenchman."

I laid hold of his legs and pulled him out. He had received no wound, and appeared to be about eighteen years of age. He most likely was frightened, as it might have been the first time he had been in action. We took him to the top of the hill where the rest of the prisoners stood with a guard around them. One of our officers, Captain Glass, could speak French; he asked them how they dared to come over in the night. They said "Their general told them there was only one company of the British in the village, and he would give each man a Spanish dollar, with a double allowance of bread and wine, if they would storm the hill!" These fellows, half drunk, were determined to give no quarter. We had killed, one officer, one sergeant, ten rank and file; wounded, one sergeant, one corporal, six rank and file. The wounded all died afterwards, save one.

We buried the officer, sergeant, and ten men in one grave. This skirmish did not last more than quarter of an hour, but it was sharp while it did last. By this time Marshal Soult had reinforced his army with a very large number of troops from France, and it was wisdom in Lord Wellington to withdraw the British army under his command out of Spain into Portugal.

We retreated by way of Almeida. This place was garrisoned by the Portuguese troops, was well-fortified with cannon, and had a high stone wall around it. We halted for the night about half a mile from the place, leaving Almeida on our right; it thundered and lightened so bad that we had never seen the like before, while the rain fell in torrents. There were neither bushes nor twigs to shelter us, so that our ammunition got wet. If we sat down, the water ran as a gutter on each side of us.

Our cavalry were posted near us. Some of them dismounted to relieve themselves from their saddles, had linked their bridles one to another, as is their usual way. The poor horses were so frightened at the dreadful thunder, that they snapped their bridles, and galloped over to the French lines, and were never recovered. This was on the 23rd of July.

At daylight we were served out with fresh ammunition, good and dry, and it was well for us we could have it, for our paymaster, early on the 24th began to muster the regiment, but could only finish two companies before the French were upon us. We had bad ground to form a line upon, and it was found necessary to move over the river, where there was a good position for artillery and infantry.

My company was an out-lying picquet, and we had to remain. We were formed into four sections; the French infantry were in line. They were so near to us that we could discern their features. They were not twenty paces from us when our officer gave the word "right about face!" As soon as we obeyed his order, we were surrounded by a troop of French hussars; they had come from behind a hill, and our company only 80 men, were thus hemmed in by horse and foot, and were all made prisoners.

Their infantry did not fire, if they had they would have killed their own hussars, who were cutting us down with their swords. Some of us fired, and thus lowered some of them. It was a great field, and very bad ground to make our retreat. There was an enclosure near us of a stone wall and a pair of gates. We made our retreat through the gates, as the hussars were cutting at us with their swords. We were so jammed up at the gateway, that they took 40 prisoners, rank and file.

The pay-sergeant, who had the company's books, and three lieutenants, (two of these officers were brothers, the present Sir Harry Smith, and his brother Thomas,) five men, and a sergeant, were wounded in making for the bridge, where the light division had crossed the river. I carried a poor fellow on my back about half a mile, who had a musket ball through his thigh. An artillery officer, on horseback, was near the bridge; he said to me:

"Is that lad wounded?"

I said "Yes sir."

"Put him behind me on the horse;" but seeing him bleeding very much, he said "I will dismount; he shall have the saddle!"

We put him on, and I was glad to be relieved from my burden.

Our troops had a good position on high ground, and there were some stone walls for shelter. We made loop-holes as we had done before. The French made a charge to come over the bridge three different times but were prevented. It was warm work! Here poor Captain Cray, Lieutenant Riley, and the Hon. Aberthnot, were all killed and buried in one grave, with their clothes on, and without coffins!

Our artillery had got their guns on rising ground, with a good range, and well served; they swept the enemy down as fast as they made the attempt to get over! At last an order was given to cease firing for two hours, to get the dead and wounded away on both sides. There was what I had never seen before, French and English all mixed, carrying their comrades that were wounded to the rear! Amongst the French who came on this errand of mercy, was an Irishman. He belonged to the Irish Brigade in the French service. He was a deserter from our army, and said in good English:

"Well Rifle Brigade, you will remember the 24th of July. We came to muster you this morning."

We replied, "We had been mustered early, before the action began; we have thinned your ranks pretty well, and if we had been allowed to keep on firing we should have thinned them a little more!"

He nodded his head and said "He liked the French service better than the English," and then turned away. If he had stayed until the time had expired, he would doubtless have had a ball from some of our rifles for his pert language.

Chapter 9

I saw one of my comrades in June last, that was taken prisoner at Almeida; he is now living at Hinckley, in Leicestershire; he told me he was surrounded by three French hussars, that he shot one, and parried off the swords of the other two for some time, until one of them made a blow at his head and cut his left eye out; and the other cut him on the thick part of his right arm, and being thus disabled he was compelled to surrender. He told me he was marched 1,500 miles up to the Alps.

He came to England in 1814, when peace was made, and joined the depot, and in the year 1815, he went to Waterloo, and was discharged with a pension of ninepence per day. His name is Joseph Tomlinson! He has a Waterloo medal. Thus mysterious are the dealings of Providence! Mysterious indeed.

> Then why let our minds be encumbered
> 'Bout what such poor worms may befal;
> When "the hairs of our heads are all numbered
> By Him who reigns king over all!"
> Moreover, his own book informs us,
> That "even a sparrow can't fall
> Without Him who feeds us, and warms;
> Without Him who reigns king over all.

But to return to my campaign, we were on our march for the Torres Vedus, as here were a long range of batteries and entrenchments made by the British troops, so that Marshal Soult could drive us no further; and we got good supplies from the fleet, while Soult was drove hard for want of provisions, and forced to retreat at this time.

I was requested to learn the bugle, with two more, as we had lost two buglers by death. It must be understood we had no drums nor fifes; we had two buglers to each company, and three to the two flank companies, making in number 22. We always went with the company in action. I liked it very well, as my pay was somewhat more. I made good progress, and was returned fit for duty at the end of one month.

As the enemy had retreated towards Spain, we followed as sharp as they led us, and we often had an encounter with them, as the rifles were always on the advance guard when they were on the retreat; or, it might be stated, "in action, first in and last out!"

We drove them to a place called "Ville Valle." A large river separated the two armies; and here Soult made a stand. A very long bridge crossed this river. Soult's position was a strong one. Here we lay, looking at each other five or six weeks.

Lord Wellington held a council of war with the other generals, to decide whether we should attack them or not, but Soult withdrew.

I was going on an outlaying picquet with my company to the bridge, one morning at daybreak; and while relieving the company that had been on duty the previous day and night, we perceived their camp fires almost burnt out. They had a sentinel at the foot of the bridge. We thought we saw him. An officer and six men made a rush towards him, and, to our surprise, it was a mawkin stuffed with straw, with jacket, and trousers, and cap, a long stick for a firelock, and for cross-belts pieces of English newspapers. We gave a shout and pursued them, and could not overtake them till next day. The rest of our army quickly followed.

The German hussars, and the fourth heavy dragoons soon overtook us, and the latter carried our knapsacks that we might run and keep up with their horses at full trot, which we did, and came in sight of the enemy near to a place called "Pumballe." Here was a river and a bridge. Captain Ross, with his troop of horse artillery came up, and said "A thousands pounds for a gun here!" and gave the word "unlimber." Fire three rounds of grape shot; gave the words "limber up" and galloped forward. We were running in front of the guns, the grape shot flying over our heads! On our way we had to scour a wood.

Our lieutenant said "I don't think there are any of the enemy in this wood."

I was walking near him; the words were scarcely out of his

mouth, before a musket-ball passed between his head and mine; we were in extended order. He bid me sound the double quick; we rushed into the wood and cleared it of its sharp-shooters. We then came to a plain, and the horse artillery came up again; on our advance we came to a French dragoon, his horse had been shot, and he could not extricate his leg from the horse's side; we set him at liberty, and sent him to the rear. He was a fine young man, and not wounded; he had rose from the ranks to an officer, and had his commission in his pocket.

We soon came in sight of this "Pumballe." The artillery playing their shot over our heads, the French rear guard could not get over the bridge fast enough; many of them took to the river. When we came up to the bridge they lay in heaps both killed and wounded, some with both legs shot off; we followed them to the other end of the town; they were in full retreat; we were within twenty paces of them when their officers gave the word for them to wheel into line.

They then faced us, poured a volley into our ranks, wounded several of our men, and an officer in the leg (Lieutenant Hopwood). One man near me had a ball passed through the upper lip, the roof of his mouth, and out of the back of his neck; he fell close to me. Those of us thus close to the French column had to retire to the bridge, where the poor French soldiers lay wounded.

They begged us to give them water, and we well supplied them from the river. One young lad had his foot nearly blown off, it hung by a bit of the skin; he begged me to cut it off, I did so and he thanked me!

We kept possession of the end of the town all night, and the French rear guard the other end, but no shots were exchanged.

The next morning they left the place, and when the whole of our army had arrived, we went forward, and came to a large plain. Our company being relieved of outlying picquet, we formed a reserve, and were posted on a hill. The enemy formed two good lines for a grand attack; we of the reserve party had nothing to do but to look on. It was a very grand sight to see the British and Portuguese armies march on the plain, with colours flying, bands playing (horse and foot) with horse and foot artillery.

The French sharp-shooters were sent out in front of their lines, their cavalry on their two flanks appeared very warlike; but when the charge was made by the British, their front line gave way, and they retreated! The man I just named, who had the ball through the roof of his mouth, we found in an out-house. The French doctor had dressed his wounds very nicely, but being unable to march, they left him. His name was John Ibbertson; he never could speak plain after. He was sent to England with some others who were wounded, and was discharged with a pension of 1/- per day; I saw him in London before I passed the board at Chelsea Hospital.

Chapter 10

We followed the enemy very close; and on the 15th of March, 1811, we had another brisk engagement. We were encamped very near the French lines; it had been a very heavy fog, and our general did not apprehend we were so near them; the fog began to clear off; I was talking with one of my comrades (our faces were not far apart) when a musket-ball passed between us, and the wind of the ball made us draw our heads back a little, the bugle sounded the assembly, and we had a warm afternoon's work.

We forced the enemy to shift their camp ground, with the loss of a great deal of baggage, wounded, and prisoners. Their mules and donkeys were ham-strung, as they had not time to get them over the river. We had several men wounded, and ten killed, in driving them out of Portugal into Spain!

I fell of the fever and was conveyed to a large place called Coimbro, and was put into a hospital for three weeks, with a great many more, sick and wounded; the treatment the doctors used soon restored me, so that I was able to join the forces. Lieutenant Hopwood, who was wounded at Pumballe, was in this place; I found him and his servant, with more wounded and sick officers in a large convent. I paid him a visit, he was upon crutches; I wished him to advance me a dollar, to purchase some tabacco.

He said "I will if you will stay with me and groom my horse, you are not well enough to join the army."

I said "I would rather go."

Then he said "you will go without your dollar!" so I was compelled to comply. I was with him one month. I left and joined the army in Spain.

The next engagement was at a place called "Cuentos D'onore." This village was taken and retaken by us and the French several times. Here was work for the bayonet! And a hard struggle for two hours and a half. The enemy were driven and defeated with great loss. Our loss was considerable.

The French retreated towards Madrid, where Soult augmented his army. He marched towards us again with a much stronger force; and we retired to the hills of Busaco, as it was a good position. A small village at the foot of these hills was occupied by the enemy; our lines extended near two miles. The enemy charged the hills at various parts of the British lines, but could not gain a footing. Our light division was posted on the left of the whole line. Here the enemy made a grand effort to crown the hill, which I really thought they would do.

Colonel Berkeley, commanding the 52nd regiment had given orders not to fire until the enemy were within ten paces. He then gave the word "fire!" and a tremendous volley was poured into them; and where the balls did no execution, the bayonet finished the work of destruction! The word "charge" was given, and they were mowed down like grass! Attacks were made at other parts of our lines, but all proved abortive; they could not move us.

I was not wanted to answer any field-call, so I sat down after this gallant charge, some 20 paces in the rear of our lines, I had worn out my shirts; the one I had on did not reach to my waist. I found a sheet in a house from which its occupants had fled; and a tailor in the regiment had cut me a shirt out of it; so here I resolved to finish it if possible. I did it, and put it on.

This engagement began about six o'clock in the morning, and was kept on until dark. We thought the enemy had been daunted, but it did not prove so, as in the morning they began as fresh as ever, and kept it up until nightfall.

When night set in, thousands deserted their ranks, and came over to us as prisoners of war. Our officers, in looking over the battle field, gave their opinion that no less than 8000 dead were left on the ground, besides their wounded, which must have amounted to a greater number. Our loss was not very great, as we had a good position, and our artillery were well served. No cavalry were engaged.

The enemy made a movement on the British in the morning of the third day, but we retreated through Coimbro with the enemy's advanced guards close at our heels. We hoisted a black flag on the convent which we occupied as a hospital, where our sick and wounded were left with a doctor to attend them, and the enemy had possession of the city! An arch of the long bridge that crossed the river we blew up, and so prevented them from chasing us. Although we were well drilled to long marches, and often had to fight with empty bellies, we had no complaining; as officers and men had to fare alike, except that captains and field officers were mounted on the march!

> Old Satan! why thus make this havoc
> Of the lives of poor mortals on earth?
> O tell us, then, proud harsh destroyer
> Why is it thou thus goest forth,
> To cut off the people in thousands,
> By bayonet, cutlass, and ball?
> Show thy power, O thou king of the nations;
> Or he shortly will murder us all!

Chapter 11

We next took our position near a large town called "Ciudad Rodrigo," which was well fortified with cannon, mounted on a high stone wall; we occupied this place in Sir John Moore's time. It was then garrisoned by the Spanish troops, but they had cowardly given it up to the French.

We lay in the villages round this place, an order was given to storm the town as soon as our battering train could be got up. At this period, we were bad off for provisions, and were troubled with a few cowardly soldiers, who, not liking to be pinched with hunger, deserted to the enemy. They little thought the town would be stormed and taken, but so it was. We broke up the ground, made our entrenchments, erected our batteries, and mounted our 42-pounders, and in the space of 14 days we effected two breaches, and on the 19th of January we took it by storm in the space of fifteen minutes.

My regiment was formed behind a convent about 300 paces from the right breach; we had made a wide ditch from this convent in the night by our working party that led straight to the breach, and the enemy had a 6-pounder at the top of it. The moon had risen, the word was given to form sections and double-quick time; off we started, the 6 pounder was loaded with grape shot and fired off, and our general Robert Crawford was killed. Some of us got up to the gun, it was loaded again, and the French gunner was in the act of applying the match, when one of our men knocked him down with the butt of his rifle. If we had been one moment later many of us would have been sent into eternity, as we were close up to the muzzle.

Some of our men on the ramparts run down to the other breach, among these was my captain; the enemy there had sprung a mine. The 5th regiment was entering when the explosion took place, and many poor fellows were blown into the air; one of them the captain, he lived only three days, his name was Uniack, an Irish gentleman, the best runner in the regiment, and one of the cleverest men than ever walked in a pair of boots. He said, just before he died, "Remember, I was the first man that entered the breach."

I ran down the main street with some more men; we met one of our officers with the French commander as a prisoner. As we passed them I heard the general say to our officer, in English:

"Where is Lord Wellington?"

The other made answer and said "You shall soon see his lordship!"

A little further in the street we met a sergeant of ours with one of our men who had deserted to the enemy. In this place the enemy had all given themselves up as prisoners of war, and among them about 40 who had deserted from the British. The French prisoners were escorted to Lisbon; and shipped for England; but these 40 were sent to the divisions and tried by court martial, for reasons before stated, and three weeks after were shot; seven of them belonged to the light division. At their execution "The Dead March in Saul" was played by the band, the caps were drawn over their faces, and the firing party, at the signal finished the work, with the lives of these traitors to their country and their king, as a warning to all others who might be disposed to join an enemy, after having sworn allegiance to their rightful sovereign.

After this shocking scene, we had orders to march to storm Badajos, a frontier town in Spain. We had more than 100 miles to march through part of Portugal and Spain. On our way we arrived at a large fortified town called "Elvas," a frontier in Portugal, only 12 miles from Badajos. At Elvas we stayed two days on our march; we had to cross a river called "Guadiana;" the bridge was composed of boats chained together. We marched from Elvas in the afternoon of the 17th of March, 1812, and arrived safe on the ground where we had to make our entrenchments.

It was dark, and the French did not perceive us; 2000 tools had been laid on the ground to work with; we worked hard, and by daylight in the morning we were safe under cover; we were relieved off duty and other troops took our place.

Next day we had to break ground in open daylight; each man

had to carry a skip and a spade; we set our skips about three paces apart, and began to fill them with earth to make a cover for us from the enemies fire; their musket balls reached us, we had two or three men wounded and one officer but no one killed. Other skips were brought to fill up the intervals and set one upon another and filled with earth, so that we soon had a good shelter from the enemies balls. We quickly had some of our batteries made and 42-pounders mounted on them.

On the 25th we opened six batteries with 28 pieces of cannon, and having kept up a heavy fire during the day on fort Picurina, when it became dark a detachment of 500 men under the command of General Kemp were ordered to storm it. They were formed into three parties, who attacked it at three different places at the same time, and they succeeded in gaining possession of it; 200 men garrisoned the place, out of which 60 were killed or drowned in the overflow of the river.

The colonel commanding, three other officers, and 86 men we took prisoners, and seven cannon were found in this fort besides some stores. In this affair we lost a great many officers and men; some of them after the fort was taken, the enemy having bombarded the fort from the town. During this time the weather was so bad with the heavy rain that the men had to work up to their knees in mud, and the river swelled to such a height that the pontoon bridge over which we crossed the Guadiana was carried away.

On the 31st of March the second parallel of batteries were completed, and 27 pieces of cannon placed on the walls of the town, and the firing was continued with great effect until the 4th of April, when another battery of six guns was opened. The breaches were effected on the 5th, and we turned out to storm the town that night, but the enemy having made formidable preparations for the defence, the attack was delayed until the next night, during which time all our guns were brought to bear upon the breaches.

The forlorn hope was composed of 350 men of the 43rd, 52nd, and Rifle Brigade, all volunteers, and two buglers from each regiment. Our bugle major made us cast lots which two of us should go on this momentous errand; the lot fell on me and another young lad. But one of our buglers who had been on the forlorn hope at Ciudad Rodrigo offered the bugle major two dollars to let him go in my stead. On my being apprised of it, he came to me, and said:

"West will go on the forlorn hope instead of you,"

I said "I shall go where my duty calls me." He threatened to confine me to the guard tent. I went to the adjutant, and reported him; the adjutant sent for him, and said:

"So you are in the habit of taking bribes;" and told him "He would take the stripes off his arm if he did the like again!" He then asked me "If I wished to go?"

I said "Yes, sir."

He said "Very good," and dismissed me.

Those who composed this forlorn hope were free from duty that day, so I went to the river, and had a good bathe; I thought I would have a clean skin whether killed or wounded, for all who go on this errand expect one or the other.

At nine o'clock at night, April 6th, we were paraded; it was then dark, and half-a-pound of bread and a gill of rum were served out to each man on parade. The party was commanded by Colonel M'Cloud of the 43rd regiment, Major O'Hare of the rifles, and Captain Jones of the 52nd regiment. We were told to go as still as possible, and every word of command was given in a whisper. I had been engaged in the field about 26 times, and had never got a wound; we had about a mile to go to the place of attack, so off we went with palpitating hearts. I never feared nor saw danger till this night.

As I walked at the head of the column, the thought struck me very forcibly "You will be in hell before daylight!" Such a feeling of horror I never experienced before! On our way to the wide ditch that surrounded the wall of the town, were laid small bags filled with grass, for each man to take up as he passed along to throw into the ditch to jump on, that we might not hurt or break our legs as the ditch was eight or nine feet deep; a party were in the rear with short ladders to be put into the ditch, and to be carried across for the men to ascend to the surface near the wall.

We had to pass between our batteries and the town; the artillery were firing blank cartridges, while we passed the guns; this we were apprised of, as being designed to keep the enemy from suspecting that we were to storm that night. There was no firing from the enemy until we arrived at the ditch. All had been still so far, but as the bags were thrown and the men descended, the enemy threw up blue lights; we could see their heads, and they poured a volley down upon us.

I was in the act of throwing my bag, when a ball went through the thick part of my thigh, and having my bugle in my left hand, it entered my left wrist and I dropped, so I did not get into the ditch. I scarcely felt the ball go through my thigh, but when it entered my wrist, it was more like a 6-pounder than a musket-ball! It smashed the bone and cut the guides, and the blood was pouring from both wounds, I began to feel very faint.

Our men were in the ditch, while the enemy had shells loaded on the top of the wall about two yards apart. As they were fired they rolled into the ditch, and when they burst, 10 or 12 men were blown up in every direction! However, some of them arrived at the breach, but a great many both killed and wounded lay around me; the balls came very thick about us, and we were not able to move. At length the whole of the light division came past me; my comrade, a sergeant, seeing me (for there was plenty of light!) said:

"Bill, are you wounded?"

I said "Yes, and cannot get up!"

He said "Here is a little rum in my flask, drink it, but I cannot assist to carry you out of the reach of shot."

His name was Robert Fairfoot. Shortly afterwards a musket ball struck him, went through the peak of his cap, and lodged in his forehead; the ball was extracted, he recovered, and through good conduct and his valour as a soldier, he obtained a commission, and was afterwards made adjutant of the regiment.

The whole of the division made for the breach; and a tremendous fire was going on. I heard our bugle-major sound the advance and double-quick. I rolled on my back (for I had fell on my side) and repeated the sound; this was the last time I blew the bugle. As another division came past me, an officer with his sword drawn stepped up to me and said:

"Desist blowing that bugle, you are drawing all the fire on my men!"

I said "I was only doing my duty!"

In a short time the firing from the wall slackened on us poor fellows that lay killed and wounded at the first onset, and those that could move got up. I was enabled through mercy to hobble to the rear, holding my left hand with my right one, as the ball had entered the joint of my wrist. I thought I was safe and out of the reach of shot from the enemy, but it did not prove so, for soon a shower of grape shot came over my head and just missed my cap.

I had moved a short distance from where I was at first, and had sat up a short time, but through loss of blood from my wounds, I was glad to lay myself down again. In a short time, four men, belonging to the band of some regiment came up to me and asked if I was wounded? I said "Yes." They had what we call a stretcher, two slant poles with a piece of sacking nailed to them for the wounded to lay on, and carried me to the doctor. These band-men were employed in this work, as they are not required to go into action. I asked them "If they could give me a drink of water?" They replied "They had none."

One of them said "There is some a little way off, but there are both dead men and horses in it, you cannot drink it."

I replied "my good fellow, run and fill your canteen."

It held about three pints; I drank it off. He ran and filled it again; I then got into the stretcher, they carried me shoulder high, and at the distance of about a mile we reached the tents, where there were about 50 staff and regimental doctors. I was so thirsty that I had emptied the three other pints before they set me down.

Chapter 12

I hobbled into the tent, there was a doctor standing by the tent-pole, with his coat off, a pair of blue sleeves on, and a blue apron; a large wax taper was burning, and there was a box of instruments laying by his side. The tent was full of wounded, all laying with their feet towards the pole; it was an awful sight to see, and to hear their groans was truly heart-rending. I stepped up to the doctor, he saw the blood trickling down my leg, and tore off a piece of my trousers to get at the wound, which left my leg and part of my thigh bare. He then made his finger and thumb meet in the hole the ball had made, and said "The ball is out my lad!" He put in some lint and covered the wound with some strapping, and bid me lay down and make myself as comfortable as I could, saying:

"There are others who need dressing worse than you!"

I said "I have another wound in my wrist," so he cut the back part of my wrist, about an inch and half, put in an instrument and pulled out a piece of the thumb bone, about half an inch long, which had been broken off by the ball, and driven to the back of the wrist. The ball could not be extracted. He then dressed the wound, and bid me lay down outside the tent as there was no room inside.

When I was out, a corporal of my company who had got a musket-ball in his shoulder, bid me try to walk with him to our own tents, about a mile off. I was willing to go with him as there was no shelter or cover we could get under. I made the attempt, but before we had walked 20 paces, my thigh being bare of covering, the bleeding had parted the lint and the strapping from the wound.

The night was very cold, so that every step I took was like a penknife in the wound, and I was two hours going the mile. On our way we passed a group of soldiers' wives, who asked us "Have our troops got into Badajos?" We told them "We feared not, and thought they never would!"

The firing was going on very sharp on both sides, and the storming lasted from nine o'clock till midnight! Our troops were driven from the breaches many times, and it was not to be wondered at; they climbed up the breaches like lions, but before they could gain a footing on the top, they were driven down into the ditch, as the enemy had every advantage over them. They had a pair of gun-wheels, with an axle-tree stuck full of swords and bayonet blades crossed, and two Frenchmen at each wheel so that when a section of our men had nearly gained the top of the breach, this instrument of death was pushed down into the ditches; and when that was gone, they had others ready.

This work of bloodshed was carried on until General Sir Thomas Picton took his division, (the 4th) round to the Castle. Scaling-ladders were made ready and planted; the enemy had no guard near the castle; the wall was about thirty-five feet high; about 80 or 100 poor fellows reached the top; others mounted the ladders with their bayonets fixed. When those lion-hearted men reached the top and had made their landing good, they gave a shout; and the enemy, hearing the noise, ran from both the breaches, poured a shower of shot into them, and on the ramparts killed or wounded almost every man that was over, and pushed down the ladders on the right hand and on the left as our men were ascending.

A man of the 30th that was in the hospital, and in the same ward with me, had no less than 13 bayonet wounds in various parts of his body when the enemy dashed the ladders down; he stripped every morning, the doctor dressed his wounds, and by good treatment he got well.

While the enemy were at this murderous work at the castle, our brave men entered both the breaches; and charged the enemy on the ramparts. When the French governor, Philipon found the Castle was taken, he retreated to Fort Christoval, and at daylight in the morning of the 7th of April, he surrendered, with all the garrison; it had consisted of 5000 men, but 1200 were killed in the assault!

After the firing ceased, our troops began to bury the dead and get the wounded to the hospital camps, where the doctors were cutting off legs and arms and dressing wounds for three successive days! No less than 17 officers of my regiment were killed near the breach. These officers were taken out of the ditch and laid on the bank side like so many dead pigs. What a black catalogue is here of the deeds of monsters in human shape, instigated to their bloody work by the arch destroyer; nevertheless, every faithful man will say:

> "I shall go where duty calls me,"
> (Motto worthy of us all);
> Not regarding what befalls me
> On this round terrestrial ball,
> To our Sovereign bound by oath,
> To our Jesus bound by love,
> Active, cheerful, hating sloth,
> With glad hearts we onward move.
> "I shall go where duty calls me"
> Hark! the echo, "I'll go too;"
> Patient bearing what befalls me,
> Jesus soon will bring me through!
> Bullets, cannon balls, or death,
> Cannot hurt the better part;
> Then I'll list to what he saith,
> Till he bids me hence depart!

Chapter 13

Mercy having so far restored me as to be enabled to go about, after two days and nights being at my regiment tents, I was ordered to join the camp where the whole of the wounded were stationed.

When I arrived there the sight was sickening in the extreme, some without arms, some without legs, and others wounded in different parts, some sitting and lying down, but none walking. Lord Wellington was there, going from one to another, with his arms folded, and asking several where they were wounded. He came to me and put the same question. I said:

"Through the right thigh and the left wrist."

He shook his head and said "Poor fellow!"

I think he cried to see so many fine young men so disabled. The sight was enough to melt the hardest heart to show "bowels of mercy," and to compassionate with sympathetic feelings.

This afternoon, the 9th, the French prisoners, with General Philipon at their head, marched past us on their way to Lisbon to embark for England. They cut a very sorry figure; their clothing was shabby and their persons dirty. They glanced at us as they passed; they were guarded by our soldiers.

On the 10th all the wounded were put into carts drawn by oxen, six in each cart, to be conveyed to Elvas in Portugal, about 12 miles distant. Here we were put into convents; there was a bed for each man. This was the first night I had lain on a bed since May 24th, 1809, nearly three years; and though I had a bed there was no sleep for me. The pain of my wound (for I was not so far recovered as to be free from pain), and the groans of my wounded comrades, prevented sleep for several nights. I was well attended by the doctor, but I could eat very little. I was nine days without anything passing my bowels.

On the twelfth day from my being wounded the ball was extracted from my hand, which looked more like a soldier's three-cocked hat than a musket ball. My hand was in a bad state, and I begged the doctor to take it off. He promised me he would the next day. He was an Italian gentleman, and could only speak broken English. I was in a room with eleven others, who had either a leg or an arm taken off, and he was said to be clever in amputating a limb.

After three weeks the general doctor looked into my ward, I beckoned him with my hand, when he came and asked me what I wanted. I said:

"Do sir, if you please, take my hand off; I cannot live, it is so painful." He bid the nurse undo the bandage and take off the splints.

He looked me in the face and said, "If I were to take your hand off now you would not live two days; it is not in a fit state to be taken off."

My arm was swelled up to the shoulder nearly as thick as my thigh. He ordered brandy and bark, which being applied the swelling went down in a few days. My doctor came to me one night and said:

"Bugler, I shall take your hand off tomorrow morning at 9 o'clock."

I said, "You have told me so many times, don't tell me so any more."

He replied, "I have spoken to two English gentlemen to assist me." I felt pleased that at this time I could put confidence in him, at least I thought I might.

The nurse dressed my wound but I was in such pain that I said "You must undo my arm, you have left some of the old poultice in the wound."

She untied the bandage, and replied, "It is all right;" but in rubbing the wound with some lint a large piece of bone from the joint fell upon the floor:

I remarked, "It was that which pained me." I afterwards had a good night's sleep.

In the morning some of the men said, "Have it cut off."

Others said, "Let it be on."

At length the three doctors came.

A servant came into the ward and bid me throw the bed rug

over me, as I was wanted in the operation room where the doctors were waiting. I had made up my mind to keep my hand on, and bid the man tell the doctor to come to me. He came and was shown the piece of bone; he then flew in a passion, and exclaimed:

"You are making a fool of me, and the other two gentlemen I have brought to assist me;" and then added "You will never be worth a farthing to your king or your country any more!"

I answered, "I have done my duty as a British soldier, and do not owe either to king or country;" (I was told that for every limb that was taken off this doctor had five pounds extra above his daily pay, whether the patient lived or died.)

He said, "If you have it off you will be entitled to what is called blood money, and you will never be able to earn a penny with that hand." I felt sorry that I had ruffled his mind by not consenting to have it off; so I said:

"Well, Sir, take it off if you think it will not get well." He then again looked at the piece of bone, turned it over with his fingers, and said in a cooler tone:

"We will let it be a day or two."

I had another good night's sleep; when he came to dress our wounds next morning I was out of bed; he began to dress a man's stump, who belonged to the 5th Dragoons; his right hand had been cut off at one blow in the joint of the wrist by a French dragoon. His hand and sword fell together by the side of his horse. His stump was a long time getting well as he would not consent to have it taken off higher up his arm. The doctor looked towards my bed, and seeing I was not there, he exclaimed in a loud voice:

"Where's the bugler?"

As I stood behind him taking off the bandage I replied, "Here, sir."

He looked and said "Let it alone, sir, I shall make you wait until I have dressed all the others, your turn will be last this morning." When he had done with the others he took me in hand, and putting on the bandage said, "How is your thigh?"

I replied "It is quite well, sir, and skinned over."

He then said "You may go tomorrow with some more on the way to Lisbon, you will there get on board of a ship, for England,

and will get three days' provisions, and if you cannot walk you can ride, as there will be spring waggons and I shall be glad to get rid of you!"

At night an English woman brought a shirt she had from me to wash, I was in bed; she said

"I have sewed the other mens' shirts and yours is the last; there are two shot holes in the left sleeve." I told her that was not mine as there were no shot holes in the one I gave her to wash, mine was almost a new one. "Well," said the woman, "Let me see your jacket?" She took it off the bed, and on examination we found two shot holes in the sleeve, although on my person no marks of this kind had been discovered.

On my way to Lisbon the weather was very hot, and not seeing a doctor for two or three days together, our wounds for want of dressing were in a very bad state. A corporal of the 83rd regiment had a musket-ball in his right shoulder; he was in such pain that it was unbearable, and addressing himself to the doctor said:

"Sir, for God's sake dress my wound, I cannot live in such agony!" The doctor took from his trousers pocket a small vial of spirits, and poured some into the wound, which brought out hundreds of maggots.

"There," said he, "You will now have some ease and sleep."

Others were in a similar plight. Having had my own wounds dressed, I stood by the doctor while this was done; I have often thought of the poor fellow's words. At length we arrived at Lisbon, and embarked for Old England.

> O how endearing, and very heart-cheering,
> Was the name of the country in which I was born;
> After many a season of conflict, I reason
> To march "double quick" to the sound of my horn.

Chapter 14

Full five years I had been absent from friends, and the thought of leaving a country full of superstition and bloodshed and returning to a land where I could enjoy means in abundance calculated to cheer the heart, revived my spirits at this time, and as our ship weighed her anchor and spread her sails to the breeze, I could not help lifting up my heart to Him who could control the elements, with the hope of reaching my native shore in safety, grateful for deliverance in the time of danger, thinking of those who still had to brave the foe, as well as the thousands who had fallen in the struggle, and while a poor unworthy worm like me, though wounded, had been mercifully preserved, and now kindly permitted to sing:

Home! sweet home!
There's no place like home!

We had 24 Portuguese sheep put on board our ship for the worst cases of the wounded, and they were killed for them as they were needed. When we had been at sea about a week, we had contrary winds (steamers were not in vogue then as they are now) which occasioned our voyage to be longer than usual, for we were out at sea from the 17th of July, to the 3rd of August, (17 days) on which day we landed at Portsmouth; but very different from our voyage out, for as stated before, we were only four days and nights going from Spithead to Lisbon! Thus Providence pleased to try our faith and patience a little, that in the end we might praise him the more.

Through this long voyage, and subsisting on salt provisions, my wounds were in a very bad state. A boat came to take us over to Gosport side, and we were put into Heslar Hospital. Those of us who had two legs got into the boat without assistance, and those who had lost a leg were hoisted over the gangway into the boat in a green chair. We had a man on board belonging to the 52nd regiment who had lost his right arm above the elbow, and his left leg above the knee, both taken off in the field at one and the same time. His name was Pynau; he could not come on deck for want of assistance.

I was in the last boat that pushed off. The mate who had charge of the boat asked if they were all out. One of the sailors said:

"I do not see any more!"

"Well," said the mate "Go down between the decks and see!"

So poor Pynau was discovered and carried by this sailor in his arms and placed in the chair; he was then hoisted over the ship's side, and all eyes were fixed on this object of pity. As he was lowered down he took off his cap, and exclaimed:

"Why don't you rejoice when you see your king coming down amongst you?"

I saw the tears roll down the cheeks of some of the sailors. This man had a wife and three children in Wales. He often said during the voyage:

"I hope I shall be spared to see them again!"

Whether he did I cannot say.

When I got into hospital, a tender-hearted gentleman came to dress my wound. He said:

"My lad, this is a bad case!" I told him I had been near having it cut off in Spain, and that the salt provisions during the voyage had made it worse, so if you think, sir, that it must come off, the sooner the better. He said "I will see it again in three days."

The two following mornings he sent his servant to dress it. On the morning of the third day he came himself; I was glad to see him; he asked me how I was? He then examined the wound. I said:

"Sir, you was to tell me today whether my hand was to be taken off or not."

He smiled and said "You will keep it on."

My heart bounded with grateful affection, and I was ready to leap out of bed at the good news! I stayed here three weeks, and wrote home to my friends to let them know I had arrived. We then went to the Isle of Wight in open boats, where we were put into barracks and had to attend the hospital every day to have our wounds dressed. A gentleman whom I had never seen before waited on me. He asked me if I was in Spain under Sir John Moore?

"Yes sir," I replied, "I saw him about 15 minutes before he was wounded."

He said "He was my own brother!" I saw the tears start in his eyes as he uttered the words "My brother!"

> Ah! many a brother, husband, friend,
> Had fallen in the strife,
> Lamented in the latter end
> By many a loving wife.
> Perhaps, by many a father dear,
> By mother too, as kind
> As ever shed a briny tear,
> Or felt a tender mind!

We stayed here three weeks, and then those of us who could march sailed over to Southampton, and from thence to Chelsea. Here I had to remain 13 weeks before my turn came to pass the board at the hospital there were so many waiting.

I received £3 16s. 2d. as my share of the prize money for the capture of Copenhagen in 1807. I was finally examined on the 8th of December, 1812. On the 9th I passed the board and was pensioned off with 9d. per day. For this I felt thankful and made the best of my way home as nearly five years had elapsed since I had seen many of my friends. When I had arrived within two miles of my native place I called at a public-house to get some refreshment as I had walked a good distance; a man was there I knew well, but he had no knowledge of me, as I was in regimentals. He asked me if I was going to Lutterworth?

I replied, "Yes." After walking on, and when we drew near to the end of our journey, I made myself known to him; it was near dark. I said "If you will go with me to a certain public-house I will treat you with a pot of beer, provided you will not mention my name." To this he agreed.

I had taken the sling off my neck and put my wounded hand into my bosom and we both sat down; I asked for a pot of beer.

The landlord said "You mean a quart."

I said "Yes, if you please. How much is it sir,"

"Ninepence" was his reply. Alas! I had only eightpence. He said, "Well, as you are a soldier I shall charge you but eightpence."

There were nine or ten drinking in the room, I knew them all; one of them asked me "what regiment?" I told him.

He said, "There are five or six from this place in your regiment." He named one.

I replied, "He is dead;" another, I said "he was killed;" a third, "He is still living!" He then mentioned myself. "Yes, I saw him in London on Thursday;" this was on Saturday. I said, "He has a father living in this place and I have a message for him."

One of them jumped up and replied, "I'll go for him;" so my father came.

A person said "This is the young man's father."

I said "Is your name Green?"

He replied "Yes," "And you have a son in the Rifles?"

"Yes!"

"Well then I saw your son on Thursday, you may expect him home the latter end of next week."

"Drink, sir, if you please." He had his eye upon me, and sat some time, then said "My name is Green, and your name is Green, and you are my son!" This conversation surprised those who had been asking me of the welfare of those who were in the regiment with me. I had engaged a bed at this house for the night, but my father said, "Let us go home."

I tried to deceive the old man but could not. If he had not seen me on furlough five years before I feel persuaded I should have had the advantage of him.

> When absent from friends for a number of years,
> We may sometimes deceive them, at least for a time,
> But a family feature, at side glance, appears
> Quite visible still, even when past our prime.
>
> Red coats or grey trousers, or even a cap,
> May deceive for a time; but the keen piercing eye
> Of a father or friend - in the wandering chap,
> Some lineal marks of close likeness will spy.

Just so in our Father's great family here,
Some family likeness distinctly we trace;
And, in prospect of home we each other can cheer,
Who are subjects of saving, enlightening grace.

Especially when His regimentals we wear,
When we all of us own as our Saviour and King;
When accoutred and clad in his robes we appear,
We may all of us shout and melodiously sing!

And when we have done with our buffetings here,
With our fightings without, and our fearings within,
We shall all meet together in harmony where
We shall be free from strife, sorrow and sin!

Chapter 15

My wounds even at this time were far from being healed owing to the bone of my arm being fractured; 29 pieces of bone of different sizes were taken out of it, and it did not thoroughly heal until 1813, about 13 months from the time I was wounded; my wrist is yet very stiff, and I cannot now either close or open my hand; a small portion of the ball is still remaining in it, which will in all probability descend to the grave with me as I have no desire to have it extracted now.

I had not been at home with my friends more than a month when an order was issued from the war office for all pensioners receiving under one shilling per day to appear for inspection. I appeared at Birmingham, where the pensioners met from four different counties; and those who were pronounced by the doctor to be fit to serve on garrison duty had to be enrolled or give up their pension, and many did so who had employment. I was found to be unfit for such duty, and therefore had liberty to return; we were allowed on this occasion 1s. 10d. for every ten miles we travelled from home and back by government.

When my hand was healed I could work at my trade, and being disposed to enter on a married state about nine months after I was discharged I took unto myself a wife. Having laid by tippling, I soon became comfortable in circumstances; my thoughts were very often at the seat of war; I also often dreamed about the battles in which I had been engaged, which were 27 in number -- 3 in Denmark, and 24 in Spain and Portugal.

I attended a place of worship and thought how good I had become since I left the army, and even fancied that I was making up past arrears of gratitude for the Lord's goodness in delivering me from war and bloodshed. I was proud of my religion, and was esteemed by others who professed it; I worked hard to get a good name, and at length the Lord opened my eyes and convinced me that my heart was not right before him, and I felt myself to be after all my professions, a wretched miserable sinner!

Hearing a good man one sabbath morning preach from these words: "Many that sleep in the dust shall awake, some to everlasting life, and some to everlasting shame and contempt," (Dan. xii. 2.) I thought if I should be found amongst the latter of these two classes what will be my doom when I leave this world, shall I be with the damned, cast out, or numbered with the blest?

But I must digress a little, and turn again to my subject. By order (in 1816) I attended at Nottingham to be examined, and there was pronounced unfit to serve; and again in 1819, at Newark, in Nottinghamshire, where I was also pronounced unfit; and here Providence smiled upon me in a most wonderful manner. A man was there belonging to my regiment who had been wounded in the arm in Spain, but was still able to serve and went out with the regiment to France, and was wounded in the leg at Waterloo. I was very much pleased to see him, he asked me if I had received any Blood money for my wounds?

I replied "No!"

He then said "You are entitled to some, I got twenty pounds."

I replied "For Waterloo! But I left in Spain therefore I had no chance."

"You have a claim on the Royal Patriot Fund, and I will put you in a way how to proceed."

I thanked him and lost no time in writing to the agents who had the management; they answered my letter, and my wound being equal to the loss of a limb, in a few weeks £15 was awarded to me on that account.

I had been discharged about seven years, and could have had it while waiting at Chelsea, but knew nothing about it. At the time it came it was very useful as trade was bad and wages low, and having a wife and three small children this made it more acceptable.

In the year 1849 I was presented with a silver medal with four bars; one for the storming of Badajos, one for Ciudad Rodrigo, one for Busaco and one for Corunna. I received 9d. per day pension for 40 years; and when the Duke of Wellington was interred a Colonel Shirley, late of the 7th Hussars being then resident at Lutterworth, sent for me and wished me to go and see his funeral; he was kind enough to pay my expenses to London and back; while I stayed in London I visited Chelsea Hospital and enquired whether any of my old comrades were there, mentioning their names; I found several, and among the rest one who had served with me in Spain and Portugal.

He asked me if I remembered Colonel Barnard?

I replied "Yes, very well, he was wounded the same night that I was at the storming of Badajos."

"Well" said my comrade, "He is now Lieutenant-governor of Chelsea Hospital: he has been wounded so many times that he can neither ride nor walk!" He further said, "As he sits at all the Boards there, it might be worth your while to wait on him."

But as I was a widower and unable to work at my trade I had not then the opportunity of doing so; however I resolved to write to him in order to solicit his kindness in laying my case before the Board and getting some addition to my pension; and in January 1853, the Lord's Commissions, &c, were pleased at his request, to allow me a pension of 1/- per day for life! Thus the Lord in his kind providence again interposed for me, and being then in my 69th year it was the more acceptable!

> But Sir Andrew has now laid his sword quite aside,
> And has done with earth's glittering pomp and his pride,
> And I hope, though he could not on earth walk or ride,
> He is numbered 'mongst those near Immanuel's side,
> Who are wearing a bright crown in glory!

> He was a most noble and kind hearted man,
> He would carry out any benevolent plan;
> On errands of mercy he often has ran,
> And when asked to do good, said "I will if I can!"
> So we hope he is landed in glory!

> Yet not on these pitiful grounds is he there!
> Oh, no! like all others, (of boasting stripp'd bare),
> One glorious robe true believers all wear,
> And in that robe Sir Andrew himself must appear,
> Stripp'd of all human merit in glory.

Chapter 16

In the same year 1853, I again entered married life; favoured with a suitable companion I changed my residence, living now in the house occupied by my present partner who had been a widow some few years in the village of South Kilworth, a little more than four miles from Lutterworth, since which period we have usually spent our sabbaths together in the town where the word of life is administered to us by our present pastor, Mr R. D'Fraine, to whom we feel strongly attached, as also to the members of the church to which we ourselves belong, reposing our trust in a bleeding Saviour.

We march our four miles to and from Lutterworth with cheerful hearts, while Jesus himself brightens our path to the blissful region where storms will be hushed, where no cannons roar, where no swords nor bayonets glitter, where no mangled bodies nor broken limbs proclaim the murderous march of an enemy, where no dead or dying will be strewed in our way to interrupt our progress, but where:

> Living souls will live and reign
> Far from misery and pain;
> Living souls from sorrows free
> Reign with Christ eternally!
> Living souls through power divine
> There will in full splendour shine;
> Living souls, from sin set free,
> There will dwell eternally!
> Living souls will shout and sing
> Praises to their heavenly King;
> In that happy world quite free,
> Then through all eternity!

Before closing my narrative, which I earnestly hope may be useful to some, I would mention, to the praise of my Heavenly friend, some few incidents to my short journey through this wilderness, which relate to His wonderful interposition in preserving a poor earthly creature from dangers and death.

In addition to all his kindness manifested during this 10 years campaign, I would notice that when about six years of age I fell into a river in the time of a flood and was carried down the stream two or three hundred yards, when I was pulled out of the mill-dam by another boy. On another occasion, I was pushed into a deep water, and was helped out at the time also, as I had not learned to swim. Once while young I was thrown from a horse and lay senseless in a field, how long I cannot say as no one was near me. When I was in my eighth year I was put out to work in a brickyard to carry clay, as my friends were poor.

On one occasion, having eat up my day's provisions I took up a small piece of bread which lay in the hovel and ate it; my master was gone to town to get drunk, as was often the case. Soon after I had eaten the bread I felt sick and giddy, so that I could not hold the riddle, to riddle the sand; the man that was tempering the clay, and another boy saw my condition; I soon became senseless, when, after a time I threw up all that I had on my stomach. On finding out that I had eaten the piece of bread, the man said that the master had put arsenic on it to poison the rats! Thus was I once more mercifully preserved from death, proving that:

"Not a single shaft can hit
Till the God of love sees fit."

Chapter 17

I will now give a faint sketch of Spain and Portugal, and the inhabitants around where I travelled.

Spain is a very mountainous country and has generally very bad roads. There are hundreds, and I believe thousands of acres of land uncultivated, and the people, especially the lower classes, are naturally lazy and filthy, as they do not boil their linen when they wash, and many of them are scarcely ever free from vermin; they are all Roman Catholics, and do not read the bible; the priests have entire control over the masses. When I was there the scriptures were a sealed book! None were allowed to read them throughout the two kingdoms except the priests.

I was once quartered with my comrade upon a priest. My comrade was a sergeant, who possessed a small bible; I used to carry it for him when on the march in my mess-kettle. I was sitting at the door one morning reading it, the priest came, looked over my shoulder, and said to me in the Spanish language:

"You have got the Holy Scriptures!"

As I could speak Spanish I replied "Yes."

He went and fetched a large bible and said, "Now, if you were a Spaniard, I should have you put into the Inquisition."

I asked "What for?"

And he replied "For being in possession of the Scriptures."

I said "Indeed! In my country there are several copies in a house!" I further remarked, "You have them!"

"Yes," said he, "We priests are allowed to have them as we explain them to the people!"

I then said "Well I am thankful I am not a Spaniard."

He then said, "You are an heretic; all heretics will go to hell when they die."

I thought his language was very insulting, especially as we were there for the purpose of driving the enemy out. I perceived he was vexed at my conversation and he at length went away in a rage. Oh,

Britains! let us prize our privileges and learn to improve them as we ought. As I was a British subject this "Wolf in sheeps clothing" had no power over me; and on this account I felt thankful.

I am happy to learn that there are now Scripture Readers in the army both at home and abroad, and sincerely hope that the Bible may find its way into that unhappy country and its truth be instilled into many men amongst that miserable people! Again I would express a hope that they may be useful to some, who, during the late war with Russia may have seen similar instances of God's care over the creatures of his own hands, and may through his blessing, lead them to a sincere and hearty consecration of all their powers to his service who is King of Kings and Lord of Lords!

Before I close I would place before the eyes of the reader, a scene after the storming of Badajos, as recorded by one of our own officers, who was an eye witness. He says:

"When I observed the defences that had been made here, I could not wonder at our troops not succeeding in the assault, the ascent of the breach near the top was covered with thick planks of wood firmly connected together, staked down, and stuck full of sword and bayonet blades, which were firmly fastened in the wood with their points up. Round the breach a deep trench was cut into the ramparts which was planted full of muskets with their bayonets standing up perpendicularly and firmly fixed in the earth up to the locks. Exclusive of this they had shell and hand grenades ready loaded piled on the ramparts, which they lighted and threw down among the assailants. Round this place death appeared in every form. The whole of the ascent was completely covered with the slain, and for many yards around the approach of the walls there was every variety of expression in their countenances, from the calm placid to the greatest agony! The sight was awful! Anxious to see the place where we had so severe a struggle, I bent my steps on the preceding evening where we had placed the ladders. Among others lay a corporal of the 45th regiment, who, when wounded, had fallen forward upon his knees and hands, and the foot of the ladder had been in the confusion placed on his back;

whether the wound had been mortal I do not know, but the weight of the men ascending the ladder had facilitated his death, for the blood was forced out of his ears, mouth, and nose! Returning to camp I passed the narrow path across the moat, where many lay dead, half in the water. I had scarcely reached the opposite side, when I perceived a woman with a child at her breast and leading another by the hand, hurrying about apparently with a distracted air, from one dead body to another, eagerly examining each. I saw her come to one whose appearance seemed to strike her, he was a grenadier of the 83rd regiment. She hesitated some moments, as if afraid to realize the suspicion which crossed her mind; at length, seemingly determined to ascertain the extent of her misery, releasing the child from her hand she raised the dead soldier, who had fallen on his face, and looking on his pallid features she gave a wild scream and the lifeless body fell from her arms. Sinking on her knees she cast her eyes to heaven, while she strained her infant to her bosom with a convulsive grasp; the blood had fled her face, nor did a muscle of it seem to move; she seemed inanimate, and all her faculties were absorbed in grief. The elder child looked up at her face for some time with anxiety, at last he said:

"Mother, why don't you speak to me? What ails you? What makes you so pale? O speak to me mother, do speak to me!"

A doubt seemed to cross her mind; without noticing the child, she again raised the mangled corpse, looked narrowly at the face, and earnestly inspected the mark of his accoutrements, but it was too true; it was her husband! Neither sigh, nor groan, nor tear escaped her, but sitting down she raised the lifeless body and placed his head on her knee, gazing in his face with feelings too deep for utterance! The child now draws himself close to her side and looking at the bleeding corpse which she sustained in a piteous tone inquired:

"Is that my father? Is he asleep? Why does he not speak to you? Shall I awake him for you?" And seizing his hand he drew it towards him, but suddenly relapsing his hold he cried, "Oh mother, his hand is cold; cold as ice."

Her attention had been drawn for some moments to the child; at length bursting out, she exclaimed, "Poor orphan, he sleeps never to wake again; never, no never will he speak to you, or me!" The child did not seem to understand her but he began to cry! She continued "O God my heart will burst! My very brain burns, but I cannot cry; surely my heart is hard; I used to cry when he was displeased with me, but I cannot cry when he is dead! Oh my husband, my murdered husband! Aye murdered," said she, wiping the blood that flowed from the wound in his breast. "Oh, my poor children;" drawing them to her bosom "what will become of you? Here she began to talk incoherently; "Will you not speak to your dear Ellen? Last night you told me you were going on guard, and you would return in the morning, but you did not come! I thought you were deceiving me, and I came to look for you!" She now ceased to speak, and rocked backwards and forwards over the corpse; but her parched lips and wild fixed look showed the agonised workings of her mind, while I stood not an unmoved spectator of this scene. But I did not interrupt her. I considered her sorrow too deep and sacred for commonplace consolation. A woman and two men of the same regiment who had been in search of her now came up and spoke to her, but she took no notice of them. A party who were burying the dead also joined them, and they crowded round striving to console her. I then withdrew and hastened unto the camp with my mind filled with melancholy reflection for many days. I felt a heavy weight on my mind, and even now I retain a vivid recollection of that appalling scene. But she was not a solitary sufferer; many a widow and orphan were made by the siege and storming of Badajos! Our loss amounted to 5000 men, British, killed; and nearly 2000 Portuguese troops, killed and wounded!"

Who could read this scene after the storming of the place without shedding tears? I think none but those who have hearts like steel, or as the nether millstone. I still feel a spark of martial spirit remaining, and think that if any enemy were to invade our favoured land, I would be one of the first to go out to meet the foe!

Yet I cannot but lament that so few of our population manifest that respect for an old soldier who has spilt his blood in fighting old England's battles which they ought; but I bless the Lord that:

> I've done with foes in a foreign land.
> Yet a strife is still kept up within!
> Though, with armour bright,
> And a sword held tight,
> I hope that a crown I shall win?
>
> But though I have now took up arms against sin,
> Yet I find myself weak as a worm,
> And if I give battle, and think I shall win,
> I can scarcely one good act perform!
>
> Indeed, if my captain himself was not near,
> To give power as well as the will,
> A thousand corruptions would spring from the rear,
> And front ranks of best doings would fill.
>
> I have comrades 'tis true, but they're weak like myself
> In themselves they cannot conquer one lust
> And great I seems a short insignificant elf,
> Scarce able to crawl in the dust!
>
> Master Loath to-stoop raises a battery near
> Then I'm forced to bend down on my knees,
> Yet e'en when the roar of law cannons I hear,
> He stands up in defiance of these.
>
> Through some port-hole old unbelief creeps to the mind,
> In the dark gloomy hour of the night,
> And then this great I sees how ignorant and blind,
> He is e'en midst Gospel Light!
>
> Indeed if 'twere not for one ray from the skies,
> Poor fellow! He'd sink in despair,
> Never more, never more in this dark world to rise,
> Much less to rise up in the air.
>
> But yet while he sees his great danger he feels,

(While his Captain with drawn sword stands by,)
Then he rushes on close to his enemy's heels,
And then in confusion they fly!

Though a company or a battalion may rise,
In one moment their movements He kens,
And if not cannon balls, or the sword he employs,
He can force them at once from their dens!

The stronghold of a ship, or strong fortified walls,
Or will of man, (stronger than both),
If He only gives orders immediately falls,
Though it may be exceedingly loth!

But however strongly fortified great I may be,
His forces can never withstand
The force of Omnipotence, all will agree,
In this, or in yon distant land!

As this German -- This frightful peninsular war
By His power has been brought to an end,
So the war-strife is permitted "to go
Thus far," by our captain and friend!

Poor resolute will! He can make thee submit,
He can make thee bow down to His sway.
He can make thee (though obstinate) bow at
His feet, And incline thee His laws to obey!

Letter to the Rev. Assheton Pownall

Buckingham Palace,
Nov. 30, 1857

 Major General Grey presents his compliments to the Rev. Assheton Pownall; and, in acknowledging the receipt of his note addressed to His Royal Highness the Prince Consort, on behalf of Pensioner William Green, begs the favour of his kindly handing the enclosed letter to the old man, who will perhaps like receiving a direct communication of the Prince's Commands addressed to him.

 Major General Grey begs also upon the part of His Royal Highness to thank Mr Pownall for his kindness in writing for this evidently deserving old soldier.

The recipient, William Green, received from the Rev. Assheton Pownall the letter above referred to from His Royal Highness with £5 enclosed; much to his sorrow he had the misfortune, after some time to lose the letter, which he would have been glad to have preserved.

A copy was forwarded to the Prince of Wales through the kindness of J. Stafford, Esq, the then Mayor of Leicester, and through the Prince's Secretary, forwarded to J. Stafford, Esq, a letter and a cheque for £3 for the old vetran.

Letter to William Green

9 Clarges Street, W.
Jan. 9th, 1860.

William Green

I write to say that your letter arrived this morning, and that it has gratified us to hear from you. I have not been able to read your letter to my father, for he is now in his 98th year, and is not able to recollect or understand anything, or else it would have given him pleasure to have heard that you remembered him for he was the very person who dressed your hand in 1812. He was then a surgeon, and offered his services to attend the wounded soldiers at Portsmouth; and he went over to the Isle of Wight one day. This my mother remembers, for she was with him.

We read your book of travels with great interest. It was brought to us by Mr Parry, a friend of Mr Lievres; and your mention of my uncle, Sir John Moore, was very affecting, for though I was only five years of age then, yet I remember the news of the battle of Corunna, and of our sad loss, coming perfectly well. Your mention of my father was also very curious. I will keep the Testimonial you have sent, which is very honourable to you. And now I beg to send you the kind wishes of all my family, who must always feel warmly to an old soldier, and hoping the rest of your life may be easy and comfortable.

I remain,

Your sincere well-wisher,

Julia Moore

Letter

Horse Guards,
November 6th, 1857.

Sir,-

I am directed by the Duke of Cambridge to acknowledge the receipt of your letter, and to say that His Royal Highness will have much pleasure in taking a copy of William Green's book, and to send you the enclosed Post Office Order for £1, which I shall feel much obliged by your forwarding to him.

Your obedient servant,

T. F. Clifton, Lt.-Col.

Letter

South Kilworth Rectory,
August 5th, 1858.

William Green, the writer of a narrative of ten years campaigning in the Peninsula, is an inhabitant of this parish, and I bear willing testimony to the good character he has obtained for himself. That any persons who may wish to help an old soldier, by purchasing the little book he has written, may have the satisfaction of knowing that he is well deserving, I have given him this testimonial.

Assheton Pownall
Rector of South Kilworth

Harry Smith

The Personal Experiences of Harry Smith,
an Officer of the 95th (Rifles), During the
Peninsular & Waterloo Campaigns
of the Napoleonic Wars
(Selected extracts from the author's autobiography)

Introduction

The following text is an account of Harry Smith's service as an officer of the Rifles during the Penninsular and Waterloo campaigns.

Unlike some of the officers and men of the 95th, Smith did not leave us a Napoleopnic memoir *per se*. He wrote a comprehensive autobiography of his entire career, which was a long and distinguished one in the Americas, Europe, India and Africa. Fortunately, the story of his life begins, as a young man, with the account that follows.

Some of the men and officers of the Rifles who had fought in Spain were sent to America to fight in 'The War of 1812' against the United States. Though not present from the outset Smith was one of those officers. He took part in the Battle of Bladensburg, the capture of Washington and the Battle of New Orleans. Whilst these were significant episodes in Smith's career, they have no part in the story that follows, which confines itself solely to the conflict against Napoleonic France.

Without seeking to change, in any way, the tone of what Smith has to tell us, we have selected the text so that it here focuses on his exploits during the Napoleonic Wars. In the interests of clarity the following have been omitted:

1. References to people and events that would not have been known to Smith at the time of the Napoleonic Wars.

2. Smith's meeting with his Spanish wife Juana was a significant episode in his life and their love story is the subject of Georgette Heyer's novel *The Spanish Bride*; but neither the story of their relationship nor the substantial religious references that accompany it are relevant to this account of his early military experiences. Where Juana appears during these experiences she, of course, remains.

3. In his autobiography Smith dwells on the death of his

mother which occurs while he is on active service; whilst reflecting on their close relationship he relates again events that he has already reported. These repetitions have been removed.

4. The autobiography was written for a contemporary audience at the time it was published and makes reference to events that had not taken place at the time of the Napoleonic wars, these references have been removed.

Leonaur Ltd

Chapter 1

Montevideo and Buenos Ayres

I was born in the parish of Whittlesea and county of Cambridgeshire in the year 1787. I am one of eleven children, six sons and five daughters. Every pains was taken with my education which my father could afford, and I was taught natural philosophy, classics, algebra, and music.

In 1804 the whole country was en masse collected in arms as volunteers from the expected invasion of the French, and being now sixteen years of age, I was received into the Whittlesea troop of Yeomanry Cavalry, commanded by Captain Johnson. During this year the Yeomanry in the neighbourhood patrolled through Norman Cross Barracks, where 15,000 French prisoners were kept, when the Frenchmen laughed exceedingly at the young dragoon, saying, "I say, leetel fellow, go home with your mamma; you most eat more pudding."

In the spring of 1805 the Whittlesea Yeomanry kept the ground at a review made by Brigadier-General Stewart (now Sir W. Stewart) when I was orderly to the General, who said, "Young gentleman, would you like to be an officer?" "Of all things." was my answer. "Well I will make you a Rifleman, a green jacket," says the General, "and very smart." I assure you the General kept his word, and upon the 15th [8th?] May, 1805, I was gazetted second lieutenant in the 95th Regiment Riflemen, 2 and joined at Brabourne Lees upon the 18th of August. A vacancy of lieutenant occurring for purchase, my father kindly advanced the money, and I was gazetted lieutenant the 15th September [August?], 1805. This fortunate purchase occurred when the 2nd Battalion of the corps was raising and the officers had not been appointed by which good luck twenty-seven steps were obtained by £100.

In the summer of 1806 a detachment of three Companies was directed to proceed from the 2nd Battalion of the corps from Faversham to Portsmouth, there to embark and form part of an army about to proceed to South America under the command of Sir Samuel Auchmuty. This detachment was under the command of Major Gardner, and I was appointed Adjutant, a great honour for so young an officer. The army sailed for America, touching at Plymouth, Falmouth, Peak of Teneriffe, and Rio Janiero, at which place it stayed one week to take in water, stores, etc., and, covered by the detachment of Riflemen, landed within a few miles of Monte Video upon the 16th of January, 1807. Some skirmishing took place the whole day with the light troops of the enemy. Upon the 17th and 18th the army halted for the artillery, stores, etc., to be landed. The outposts (Riflemen) were employed both of these days.

Upon the 19th the army moved forward, and a general action took place, the result of which was most favourable to the British, and a position was taken up in the suburbs of Monte Video. Upon the 20th the garrison made a most vigorous sortie in three columns, and drove in our outposts, and a heavy and general attack lasted for near two hours, when the enemy were driven to the very walls of the place. The Riflemen were particularly distinguished on this occasion.

The siege of Monte Video was immediately commenced and upon the morning of the 3rd of February, the breach being considered practicable, a general assault was ordered in two columns, the one upon the breach, the other an escalade. Both ultimately succeeded. Not a defence was destroyed nor a gun dismounted upon the works. The breach was only wide enough for three men to enter abreast, and when upon the top of the breach there was a descent into the city of twelve feet. Most of the men fell, and many were wounded by each other's bayonets. When the head of the column entered the breach, the main body lost its communications or was checked by the tremendous fire. Perceiving the delay, I went back and conducted the column to the breach, when the place was immediately taken. The slaughter in the breach was enormous owing to the defence being perfect, and its not being really practicable. The surrender of this fortress put the English in the possession of this part of the country.

I was now afflicted with a most severe fever and dysentery, and owe my life to the kind attentions of a Spanish family in whose house I was billeted. My own relations could not have treated me with greater kindness. My gratitude to them can never be expressed or sufficiently appreciated.

In the autumn an outpost was established on the same side of the river as Monte Video, but nearly opposite to Buenos Ayres, at Colonia del Sacramento. This had formerly belonged to the Portuguese. It was situated on a neck of land, and a mud wall was carried from water to water. There were no guns up, and in one place a considerable breach. One particular night a column of Spaniards which had crossed the river from Buenos Ayres stormed this post, and were near carrying it by surprise had it not been for the valour of Scott and his guard of Riflemen, who most bravely defended the breach until the troops got under arms. The enemy were not pursued, as their numbers were not known and the night was dark. Why this breach was not repaired one cannot say, except that in those days our commanders understood little of the art of war, and sat themselves down anywhere in a state of blind security without using every means to strengthen their posts. Experience taught us better.

The enemy did not re-cross the river, but took up a position about fourteen miles from Colonia, in which Colonel Pack (afterwards Sir Dennis Pack), who commanded the British force, resolved to attack them. The column consisted of three companies of Riflemen, the 40th Regiment, two 6-pounders, and three light companies. It marched upon the night of [6-7 June], and arrived in sight of the enemy at daylight in the morning. They were drawn up on an elevated piece of ground, with a narrow but deep, muddy, and miry river in their front. Their cavalry formed a right angle upon the right of their infantry and they had seven guns upon the left. The Rifle Brigade covered the troops whilst crossing the rivulet, and in about twenty minutes by a rapid advance the position was carried, the enemy leaving behind him his guns, tents, stores, etc., with a great quantity of ammunition. In the destroying of the latter poor Major Gardner and fourteen soldiers suffered most dreadfully from an explosion. Some flints had been scattered upon the field; the soldiers took the shot to break the cartridges and thus the whole blew up. About two hundred shells also exploded. The army at a short distance lay down, and not an individual was touched. Colonel Pack, with his army, the captured guns, etc., returned to Colonia in the evening.

A considerable force having arrived under General Whitelock, who took the command, the army was remodelled and embarked in August [really on the 17th of June], 1807, to attack Buenos Ayres. The post of Colonia was abandoned, and the three companies of the 2nd Battalion Rifle Brigade were embodied with five of the 1st just arrived from England, and I was appointed adjutant of the whole under the command of Major McLeod. The army landed upon [28 June], and was divided into two columns, the one consisting of the light troops under General Craufurd, and of a heavy brigade, the whole under Major-General Leveson-Gower. His column was one day in advance of the main body commanded by General Whitelock in person. His orders were to march up to the enemy's outposts and take up a position. In place of obeying his orders, General Leveson-Gower immediately attacked the enemy in the suburbs of Buenos Ayres, and drove them in with great loss, leaving their cannon behind them. Having thus committed himself, in lieu of following up the advantage he had gained and pushing forward into Buenos Ayres, which would have immediately surrendered, he halted his column and took up a position. The enemy recovered from his panic, and with the utmost vigour turned to and fortified the entrances of all the streets. (Buenos Ayres is perfectly open on the land side, but has a citadel of some strength within the town and upon the river. The houses are all flat-roofed, with a parapet of about three feet high.) The day after the affair alluded to, General Whitelock with his column arrived. The next day he reconnoitred the enemy, drove in their outposts, and partially invested the city. Some very heavy skirmishing took place in the enclosures, the fences consisting of aloe hedges, very difficult to get through, but making excellent breastworks. The Rifle Corps particularly distinguished themselves.

Upon the [5 July] the whole army attacked in four columns. The men were ordered to advance without flints in their muskets, and crowbars, axes, etc., were provided at the head of the column to break open the doors, which were most strongly barricaded. It must be stated that the streets of Buenos Ayres run at right angles from each other. Each street was cut off by a ditch and a battery behind it. Thus the troops were exposed to a cross fire. The tops of the houses were occupied by troops, and such a tremendous fire was produced of grape, canister, and musketry, that in a short time two columns were nearly annihilated without effecting any impression. The column I belonged to, under Brigadier-General Craufurd, after severe loss, took refuge in a church, and about dusk in the evening surrendered to the enemy. Thus terminated one of the most sanguinary conflicts Britons were ever engaged in, and all owing to the stupidity of the General-in-chief and General Leveson-Gower. Liniers, a Frenchman by birth, who commanded, treated us prisoners tolerably well, but he had little to give us to eat, his citadel not being provisioned for a siege. We were three or four days in his hands, when, in consequence of the disgraceful convention entered into by General Whitelock, who agreed within two months to evacuate the territory altogether and to give up the fortress of Monte Video, we were released. The army re-embarked with all dispatch and sailed to Monte Video. Our wounded suffered dreadfully, many dying from slight wounds in the extremity of lockjaw.

The division of troops I belonged to sailed upon [12 July], under the command of Brigadier-General Lumley. I confess I parted from the kind Spanish family, who during my illness had treated me with such paternal kindness, with feelings of the deepest sorrow and most lively gratitude. The old lady offered me her daughter in marriage and $20,000, with as many thousand oxen as I wished, and she would build me a house in the country upon any plan I chose to devise.

The fleet separated in a gale of wind off the Azores. During this gale the transport I was in carried away its rudder. Our captain had kept so bad a reckoning we ran four hundred miles after he expected to make the Lizard. In the chops of the Channel we fell in with the Swallow, sloop of war, to whom we made a signal of distress, and she towed us into Falmouth Harbour [5 Nov.] It blew the most tremendous gale of wind that night. A transport with the 9th Dragoons aboard was wrecked near the Lizard, and this would inevitably have been our fate had we not been towed in by the sloop of war. The rudder was repaired, we were driven into Plymouth, and in the middle of December anchored at Spithead, where we delighted to have arrived. However, to our great mortification, we were ordered to the Downs, there to disembark.

I obtained leave of absence, and was soon in the arms of a most affectionate family, who dearly loved me.

Chapter 2

With Sir John Moore -- Battle of Coruna

I stayed in this happy land of my sires for two months, when I was ordered to join. The Regiment was then quartered at Colchester. Although there were many subalterns present who were senior to me, I had given to me, for my exertions abroad as Adjutant, the command of a Company. This was the act of my kind and valued friend Colonel Beckwith, whom I shall have occasion frequently to mention in these memoirs, but never without feelings of affection and gratitude. The Company was in very bad order when I received it, which Colonel Beckwith told me was the reason he gave it me. I now procured a commission for my brother Tom, who was gazetted over the heads of several other candidates.

In the summer [spring] of 1808 10,000 men were ordered to Sweden under the command of Sir J. Moore. Three Companies of the Rifle Brigade under Major Gilmour were to form part of the expedition. By dint of great exertion I was appointed Adjutant to this detachment. We marched to Harwich to embark. When the fleet was collected, we anchored a few days in Yarmouth roads. The fleet arrived at Gottenburgh [on 7th May], blowing a heavy gale of wind. The harbour of this place is most beautiful. The army never landed, but the men were drilled, embarking and disembarking in flat-bottomed boats. I jumped against three regiments, 95th, 43rd and 52nd, and beat them by four inches, having leaped 19 feet 4 inches.

At this period Napoleon announced his unjust invasion of Spain, and Sir John Moore's army was ordered to sail and unite with the forces collecting on the coast of Portugal for the purpose of expelling Junot's army from Lisbon. On approaching the mouth of the Mondego, a frigate met us to say Sir Arthur Wellesley's army had landed in Mondego and pushed forward, and that Sir John Moore was to sail for Peniche, and there land on arrival. The battle of Vimiera had been fought [21 Aug. 1808], and the Convention was in progress. Sir John Moore's army landed one or two days after the battle and took the outposts. The three Companies to which I was Adjutant joined Colonel Beckwith and the headquarters of the Regiment, and I was appointed to Captain O'Hare's Company (subalterns Smith, W. Eeles, Eaton).

After the embarkation of the French army, an army was formed under Sir John Moore for the aid of the Spaniards, and it moved on the frontier of Alemtejo.

The 95th were quartered in Villa Viciosa, in an elegant palace. I occupied a beautiful little room with a private staircase, called the Hall of Justice. I was sent by Sir Edward Paget to examine the fort Xuramenha and report upon it, the fords of the Guadiana, etc., near the important fortress of Badajos.

In the autumn of this year (1808), Sir John Moore's army moved on Salamanca. As I could speak Spanish, I was employed by Colonel Beckwith to precede the Regiment daily to aid the Quartermaster in procuring billets and rations in the different towns, and various were the adventures I met with. The army was assembled at Salamanca, and never did England assemble such a body of organized and elegant troops as that army of Sir John Moore, destined to cover itself with glory, disgrace, victory, and misfortune. The whole of this campaign is too ably recorded by Napier for me to dwell on. I shall only say that never did corps so distinguish itself during the whole of this retreat as my dear old Rifles. From the severe attack on our rear-guard at Calcavellos [3 Jan. 1809], where I was particularly distinguished, until the battle of Coruña, we were daily engaged with a most vigorous and pushing enemy, making the most terrific long marches (one day 37 miles). The fire of the Riflemen ever prevented the column being molested by the enemy; but the scenes of drunkenness, riot, and disorder we Reserve Division witnessed on the part of the rest of the army are not to be described; it was truly awful and heartrending to see that army which had been so brilliant at Salamanca so totally disorganized, with the exception of the reserve under the revered Paget and the Brigade of Guards. The cavalry were nearly all dismounted, the whole a mass of fugitives and insubordinates; yet these very fellows licked the French at Coruña like men [16 Jan.]. The army embarked the following day. I shall never forget the explosion of a fortress blown up by us -- the report cannot be imagined. Oh, the filthy state we were all in! We lost our baggage at Calcavellos; for three weeks we had no clothes but those on our backs; we were literally covered and almost eaten up with vermin, most of us suffering from ague and dysentery, every man a living still active skeleton. On embarkation many fell asleep in their ships and never awoke for three days and nights, until in a gale we reached Portsmouth [21 Jan]. I was so reduced that Colonel Beckwith, with a warmth of heart equalling the thunder of his voice, on meeting me in the George Inn, roared out:

"Who the devil's ghost are you? Pack up your kit -- which is soon done, the devil a thing have you got -- take a place in the coach, and set off home to your father's. I shall soon want again such fellows as you, and I will arrange your leave of absence!"

I soon took the hint, and naked and slothful and covered with vermin I reached my dear native home, where the kindest of fathers and most affectionate of mothers soon restored me to health.

Chapter 3

Back to the Peninsula under Sir Arthur Wellesley

In two months I rejoined the Regiment at Hythe. From Hythe we marched for Dover, where we embarked for Lisbon [25th May] to join the Duke's army. Having landed at Lisbon we commenced our march for Talavera. On this march -- a very long one -- General Craufurd compiled his orders for the march of his Brigade, consisting of the 43rd, 52nd, and 95th, each upwards of 1000 strong. These orders he enforced with rigour (as it seemed at the moment), but he was in this way the means of establishing the organization and the discipline of that corps which acquired for it its after-celebrity as the "Light Division."

We had some long, harassing and excessively hot marches. In the last twenty-eight hours we marched from Oropesa to Talavera, a distance of fourteen Spanish leagues (56 miles), our soldiers carrying their heavy packs, the Riflemen eighty rounds of ammunition. But the battle of Talavera was thundering in our ears, and created a spirit in the Brigade which cast away all idea of fatigue. We reached the sanguinary field at daylight after the battle [29 July], greeted as if we were demi-gods by all the gallant heroes who had gained such a victory. We took up the outposts immediately, and some of us Riflemen sustained some heavy skirmishing. The field was literally covered with dead and dying. The bodies began to putrefy, and the stench was horrible, so that an attempt was made to collect the bodies and burn them. Then, however, came a stench which literally affected many to sickness. The soldiers were not satisfied with this mode of treating the bodies of their dead comrades, and the prosecution of the attempt was relinquished. After our stay at Talavera [29 July-3 August], during which we were nearly starved, the army commenced its retreat, passing the bridge of Arzobispo in the most correct and soldier-like manner, our Brigade forming the rear-guard. The army retired on Deleytosa, the Light Brigade remaining in a position so as to watch the bridge of Almaraz. Here for three weeks we were nearly starved [6 Aug.-20 Aug.], and our position received the name of Doby Hill. We marched every evening and bivouacked so as to occupy the passage of the Tagus, and at daylight returned to our hill. Honey was plentiful, but it gave dysentery. My mess -- Leach's Company (Leach, Smith, Layton, and Bob Beckwith) -- were not as badly off as our neighbours. We had a few dollars, and as I could speak Spanish, I rode into the lines of the Spanish troops, where I could always purchase some loaves of bread at a most exorbitant price. With this and some horrid starved goats we lived tolerably for soldiers in hard times. The army retired into quarters -- the headquarters to Badajos, our Division (which had added to it Sir Rufane Donkin's Brigade, the 45th, 87th and 88th Regiments) to Campo Mayor [11th Sept.], where sickness and mortality commenced to an awful extent. On our reaching the frontier of Portugal, Castello de Vidi, wine was plentiful, and every man that evening had his skin full.

During the period we were at Campo Mayor [11th Sept.-12 Dec.], the Hon. Captain James Stewart and I got some excellent greyhounds. We were always out coursing or shooting, and were never sick a day; our more sedentary comrades many of them distressingly so. The seven right-hand men of Leslie's Company died in the winter of this year.

While at Campo Mayor the convalescents of my Light Brigade were ordered to our old fortress, called Onguala, on the immediate frontier of Portugal, and opposite to Abuchucha, the frontier of Spain. They consisted of forty or fifty weakly men. I was first for Brigade duty, and I was sent in command, with a Lieut. Rentall of the 52nd Regiment and my brother Tom, who was sick. I knew this country well, for we had had some grand battues there, and shot red deer and wild boars. So soon, therefore, as I was installed in my command, lots of comrades used to come from Campo Mayor to breakfast with me and shoot all day. On one occasion Jack Molloy, Considine, and several fellows came, and while out we fell into the bivouac of a set of banditti and smugglers. We hallooed and bellowed as if an army were near us. The bandits jumped on their horses and left lots of corn-sacks etc., in our hands; but on discovering our numbers, and that we fired no balls (for we had only some Rifle buttons pulled off my jacket), being well armed, they soon made us retreat. This, after my friends returned to Campo Mayor, so disconcerted me that I made inquiry about these same rascals, and ascertained there were a body of about twenty under a Catalan, the terror of the country. I immediately sent for my sergeant (a soldier in every sense of the word) to see how many of our convalescents he could pick out who could march at all. He soon returned. He himself and ten men, myself, Rentall, and my sick brother Tom (who would go) composed my army. I got a guide, and ascertained that there were several haunts of these bandits; so off I started. We moved on a small chapel (many of which lone spots there are in all Roman Catholic countries), at which there was a large stable. On approaching we heard a shot fired, then a great and lawless shouting, which intimated to us our friends of the morning were near at hand. So Pat Nann and I crept on to peep about. We discovered the fellows were all inside a long stable, with a railed gate shut, and a regular sentry with his arms in his hand. They were all about and had lights, and one very dandy-looking fellow with a smart dagger was cutting tobacco to make a cigar. Pat and I returned to our party and made a disposition of attack, previously ascertaining if the stable had a back door, which it had not. I then fell in our men very silently, Mr Rentall being much opposed to our attack, at which my brother Tom blew him up in no bad style of whispering abuse, and our men went for the gate. The sentry soon discovered us and let fly, but hit no one. The gate was fast and resisted two attempts to force it, but so amazed were the bandits, they [never] attempted to get away their horses, although their arms were regularly piled against the supports of the roof of the stable, and we took twelve banditti with their captain, a fine handsome fellow, horses, etc. His dagger I sent to my dear father. I sent my prisoners on the next day to Campo Mayor, galloping ahead myself, in an awful funk lest General Craufurd should blow me up. However, I got great credit for my achievement in thus ridding the neighbourhood of a nest of robbers; and the captain and five of his men (being Spaniards) were sent to Badajos and sentenced to the galleys for life, being recognized as old offenders.

The remainder received a lesser punishment. My men got forty Spanish dollars each prize money, the amount I sold the horses for. I bought for forty dollars the captain's capital horse. The men wanted me to keep him as my share, but I would not. Dr. Robb, our surgeon, gave sixty Spanish dollars for a black mare. Thus ended the Battle of the Bandits.

Chapter 4

Campaign of 1810 -- The 1st German Hussars

In the winter of this year [12 Dec. 1809] we marched towards the northern frontier of Portugal. We marched towards Almeida, and were cantoned in villages to its rear -- Alameda, Villa de Lobos, Fequenas, not far from the Douro. Here too was good shooting and coursing; but I was not permitted to be idle. We moved into Spain [19 Mar. 1810], and at Barba del Puerco had a most brilliant night attack in which Colonel Beckwith greatly distinguished himself.

At Villa de Ciervo a detachment of one sergeant and twelve Hussars (1st German) were given me by General Craufurd to go right in among the French army, which had moved on Ciudad Rodrigo and then retired. Many are the hairbreadth escapes my Hussars and I had, for we were very daring; we were never two nights in the same place. One night at Villa de Ciervo, where we were watching a ford over the Agueda, two of my vedettes (two Poles elegantly mounted) deserted to the enemy. The old sergeant, a noble soldier, came to me in great distress.

"Oh mein Gott, upstand and jump up your horse; she will surely be here directly!"

I was half asleep, with my horse's reins in my hand, and roared out, "Who the devil is she?"

"The Franzosen, mein Herr. Two d—d schlems have deserted."

So we fell back to the rear of the village, sitting on our horses the remainder of the night, every moment expecting the weakness of our party would cause an attempt to cut us off. At daylight we saw fifty French dragoons wending their way on the opposite bank to the ford. I immediately got hold of the padre and alcalde (priest and magistrate), and made them collect a hundred villagers and make them shoulder the long sticks with which they drive their bullock-carts and ploughs, which of course at a distance would resemble bayonets. These villagers I stationed in two parties behind two hills, so that the "bayonets" alone could be seen by the enemy. Then with my sergeant and ten Hussars (two having deserted) I proceeded to meet the enemy, first riding backwards and forwards behind a hill to deceive him as to my numbers. The French sent over the river about half their number. I immediately galloped up to them in the boldest manner, and skirmished advancing. The enemy were deceived and rapidly retired, and I saved the village from an unmerciful ransacking, to the joy of all the poor people.

At this period General Craufurd had officers at two or three of the most advanced vedettes where there were beacons, who had orders to watch the enemy with their telescopes, and, in case of any movement to report or fire the beacon. I was on this duty in rather a remote sport on the extreme left of our posts. The vedette was from the 1st Hussar picquet. These men would often observe a patrol or body of the enemy with the naked eye which was barely discernible through a telescope, so practised were they and watchful. Towards the evening my servant ought to have arrived with my dinner (for we officers of the look-out could take nothing with us but our horse and our telescope), but he must have missed his way, and as my appetite was sharpened by a day's look-out I began to look back, contrary to the vedette's idea of due vigilance. He asks, "What for Mynheer so much look to de rear?"

I, sad at the fast, "Hussar, you are relieved every two hours. I have been here since daylight. I am confounded hungry, and am looking out for my servant and my dinner."

"Poor yonge mans! but 'tis notings."

"Not to you," said I, "but much to me."

"You shall see, sir. I shall come off my horse, you shall up clim, or de French shall come if he see not de vedette all right."

Knowing the provident habits of these Germans I suspected what he was about. Off he got; up get I en vedette. With the greatest celerity, he unbuckled his valise from behind his saddle, and took out a piece of bacon (I had kept up a little fire from the sticks and bushes around me), from a cloth some ground coffee and sugar, from his haversack some biscuit, and spread on the ground a clean towel with knife, fork and a little tin cup. He had water in his canteen -- his cooking-tin. He made me a cup of coffee, sliced some bacon, broiled it in the embers, and in ten minutes coffee, bacon, biscuit were ready and looked as clean as if in a London tavern.

He then says, "Come off." Up he mounts, saying, "Can eat. All you sall vant is de schnaps."

I fell to, and never relished any meal half so much; appetite was perfect, and the ingenious, quick and provident care of the Hussar added another to the many instances I had witnessed of this regiment to make them be regarded, as indeed they were, as exemplary soldiers for our emulation.

My servant soon after arrived. The contents of his haversack I transferred to my kind friend the Hussar's, and half the bottle of wine, on which the Hussar remarked, "Ah, dat is good; the schnaps make nice;" and my servant put up his valise again for him. I was highly amused to observe the momentary glances the Hussar cast on me and my meal, for no rat-catcher's dog at a sink-hole kept a sharper look-out to his front than did this vedette. In the whole course of my service I never was more amused, and nothing could be more disinterested than the Hussar's conduct, which I never forgot.

Chapter 5

Campaign of 1810 -- Battle of Coa

Soon after this the French invested Ciudad Rodrigo, and regularly commenced the siege. The Light Division (into which fell the three regiments 43rd, 52nd and two Battalions of Rifles, 1st and 3rd Portuguese Caçadores, the latter under Elder, a most brilliant Rifle officer), 1st Hussars, 14th Light Dragoons, 16th Light Dragoons occupied Gallegos, Exejo, etc., our advanced post being at Marialva, on the road to Ciudad Rodrigo. During the whole siege our alerts were innumerable, and at Marialva we had several very smart skirmishes, but so able were Craufurd's dispositions, we never lost even a vedette.

The French were in the habit of patrolling over the Agueda with cavalry and infantry, about 30 Dragoons and 200 foot. General Craufurd determined to intercept one of these patrols [10 July], and [moved out with] the cavalry, 1st Hussars, 14th and 16th Light Dragoons, and Light Division. It may now be asked, Was it necessary to take out such a force to intercept so small a party? Certainly. Because the enemy might have crossed the Agueda to support the patrols. We were all moved to where directed, the infantry were halted, some of the cavalry moved on. At grey daylight the patrols of the enemy appeared, their Dragoons some way in advance of the infantry. The patrol was very incautiously conducted (not like our 1st Hussars), and the Dragoons were taken in a moment. The infantry speedily retired to an eminence above the ford and formed square. Craufurd ordered them to be attacked by the cavalry, and several right good charges were made; but the French were steady, the dead horses in their front became a defence, and our cavalry never made the slightest impression. Craufurd never moved one of us. The charges of cavalry ceased for a few seconds -- the fields around were high-standing corn. The gallant fellow in command gave the word, "Sauve qui peut." In a moment all dispersed, ran through the standing corn down to the banks of the river, and were saved without the loss of a man. The officer was promoted on his arrival in his camp.

Our loss was very considerable. Poor Colonel Talbot of the 14th (commanding) killed, and a lot of men. I and Stewart, Adjutant of the Rifle Brigade, asked leave to go ahead, and we saw it all. Indeed, it was in sight of the whole division. Had two Companies of ours only been moved to threaten the ford, the enemy would have laid down their arms. Such a piece of soldiering as that morning presented the annals of war cannot produce.

While we were at a village called Valde Mula, in the neighbourhood of Fort Concepcion, that most perfect little work was blown up [21st July]. It was the neatest fortification I ever saw (except the Moro in the Havana subsequently), and the masonry was beautifully executed.

After the fall of Ciudad Rodrigo, which made a brilliant defence, our advanced line fell back to the Dos Casas, and in front of Alameda we had a brilliant affair with the French, in which Krauchenberg 1st Hussars and McDonald Royal Artillery greatly distinguished themselves. The 3rd Caçadores were this day first under fire, and behaved nobly. After this our advanced posts were retired behind the Dos Casas to cover Almeida. While Massena prepared his army to invade Portugal and besiege Almeida, we were daily on the alert and had frequent skirmishes. General Craufurd, too, by a variety of ruses frequently made the whole French army turn out.

In the early morning of the 24th of July (I was on picquet with Leach and my Company that night) the enemy moved forward with 40,000 men. Our force, one Brigade of Horse Artillery, three Regiments of cavalry, five of infantry, were ordered by the Duke to remain as long as possible on the right bank of the Coa, where there was a bridge over the river on the road from Almeida into Portugal to Celerico and Pinhel, posting ourselves between the fortress and the bridge, so as to pass over so soon as the enemy advanced in force. In place of doing this, Craufurd took up a position to our right of Almeida, and but for Colonel Beckwith our whole force would have been sacrificed. Fortunately a heavy rain had fallen, which made the Coa impassable except by the bridge, which was in our possession, and the enemy concentrated his force in one rush for the bridge [24 July].

During the Peninsular War there never was a more severe contest. The 43rd lost 17 officers and 150 men, my Regiment 10 officers and 140 men. When we passed the bridge my section was the rear-guard of the whole, and in a rush to drive back the enemy (with whom we were frequently absolutely mixed), my brother Tom and I were both severely wounded, and a Major Macleod, a noble fellow, afterwards killed at Badajos, put me on his horse, or I should have been taken. The enemy made several attempts to cross, but old Alister Cameron, Captain in the Rifle Brigade, had posted his Company in a ruined house which commanded the bridge, and mainly contributed to prevent the passage of the enemy, who made some brilliant attempts. The bridge was literally piled with their dead and they made breastworks of the bodies. On this day, on going to the rear wounded, I first made the acquaintance of my dear friend Will Havelock, afterwards my whipper-in, who was joining the 43rd fresh from England, with smart chako and jacket. I had a ball lodged in my ankle-joint, a most painful wound. We were sent to Pinhel, where the 3rd Division was seven leagues from the action Sir Thomas Picton treated us wounded like princes.

The wounded were ordered to the rear, so as to embark on the Mondego at Pinhel. In collecting transport for the wounded, a sedan chair between two mules was brought, the property of some gentleman in the neighbourhood, and, fortunately for me, I was the only person who could ride in it, and by laying my leg on the one seat and sitting on the other, I rode comparatively easy to the poor fellows in the wretched bullock-cars, who suffered excruciating agony, poor brother Tom (who was very severely wounded above the knee) among the rest. This little story will show what wild fellows we were in those days. George Simmons' (1st Rifles) bullocks at one stage had run away. As I was the spokesman, the surgeon in charge came to me in great distress. I sent for the village magistrate, and actually fixed a rope in my room to hang him if he did not get a pair of bullocks (if the Duke of W. had known he would have hung me). However, the bullocks were got, and off we started. The bullocks were not broken, and they ran away with poor George and nearly jolted him to death, for he was awfully wounded through the thick of the thigh. However, we all got down to Pinhel [31st July], and thence descended the Mondego by boats, landing every night. At one house a landlord was most insolent to us, and Lieut. Pratt of the Rifles, shot through the neck, got very angry. The carotid artery must have been wounded, for it burst out in a torrent of blood, and he was dead in a few seconds, to our horror, for he was a most excellent fellow. On the same bed with me was a Captain Hull of the 43rd Regiment with a similar wound. I never saw any man in such a funk.

On our reaching the mouth of the Mondego, we were put on board a transport. In the ship with me was a stout little officer, 14th Light Dragoons, severely wounded, whose thigh afterwards disgorged a French 6-lb. shot. On arrival in Lisbon [7th Aug.] we were billeted in Buenos Ayres, poor Tom and I in awful agony in our miserable empty house. However, we got books, and I, although suffering, got on well enough. But poor Tom's leg was in such an awful state he was sent home. George Simmons's wound healed. My ball was lodged on my ankle-joint, having partially divided the tendo Achillis. However, we heard of the army having retired into the celebrated lines of Torres Vedras, and nothing would serve us but join the Regiment. So our medical heroes very unwillingly sent us off to Belem, the convalescent department under Colonel Tucker, 29th Regiment, a sharp fellow enough. When I, George Simmons, and Charlie Eeles, 3rd Battalion, just arrived sick from Cadiz, waited on him to express our desire to join, he said, "Oh, certainly; but you must be posted to do duty with convalescents going up the country." I was lame and could not walk. George Simmons cantered on crutches, and Charlie Eeles was very sick. However, go or no go, and so we were posted to 600 villains of every Regiment in the army under a long Major Ironmonger of the 88th (afterwards of Almeida celebrity, when the garrison escaped). We marched in a day [7 Oct.]. On the first day's march he pretended to faint. George Simmons, educated a surgeon, literally threw a bucket of water over him. He recovered the faint, but not the desire to return; and the devil would have it, the command devolved on me, a subaltern, for whom the soldiers of other corps have no great respect, and such a task I never had as to keep these six hundred rascals together. However, I had a capital English horse, good at riding over an insubordinate fellow, and a voice like thunder.

The first bivouac I came to was the guards (these men were very orderly). The commanding officer had a cottage. I reported myself. It was raining like the devil. He put his head out of the window, and I said:

"Sir, I have 150 men of your Regiment convalescent from Belem."

"Oh, send for the Sergeant-major," he very quietly said; -- no "walk in out of the rain."

So I roared out, "We Light Division men don't do duty with Sergeant-majors, nor are we told to wait. There are your men, every one -- the only well-conducted men in 600 under my charge -- and these are their accounts!" throwing down a bundle of papers, and off I galloped, to the Household man's astonishment.

That day I delivered over, or sent by officers under me, all the vagabonds I had left. Some of my own men and I reached our corps that night at Arruda, when old Sydney Beckwith, dear Colonel, said:

"You are a mad fool of a boy, coming here with a ball in your leg. Can you dance?"

"No," says I; "I can hardly walk but with my toe turned out."

"Can you be my A.D.C.?"

"Yes; I can ride and eat," I said, at which he laughed, and was kind as a brother; as was my dear friend Stewart, or Rutu, as we called him, his Brigade Major, the actual Adjutant of the Regiment.

That very night General Craufurd sent for me, and said:

"You have come from Sobral, have you not, to-day, and know the road?"

I said, "Yesterday."

"Well, get your horse and take this letter to the Duke for me when it is ready."

I did not like the job, but said nothing about balls or pains, which were bad enough. He kept me waiting about an hour, and then said:

"You need wait no longer; the letter won't be ready for some time, and my orderly dragoon shall take it. Is the road difficult to find?"

I said, "No; if he keeps the chaussée, he can't miss it."

The poor dragoon fell in with the French patrol, and was taken prisoner. When the poor fellow's fate was known, how Colonel Beckwith did laugh at my escape!

At Arruda we marched every day at daylight into position in the hills behind us, and by the ability of Craufurd they were made impregnable. The whole Division was at work. As Colonel Beckwith and I were standing in the camp one day, it came on to rain, and we saw a Rifleman rolling down a wine-cask, apparently empty, from a house near. He deliberately knocked in one of the heads; then -- for it was on the side of a rapidly shelving hill -- propped it up with stones, and crept in out of the rain. Colonel Beckwith says:

"Oh, look at the lazy fellow; he has not half supported it. When he falls asleep, if he turns round, down it will come."

Our curiosity was excited, and our time anything but occupied, so we watched our friend, when in about twenty minutes the cask with the man inside came rolling down the hill. He must have rolled over twenty times at least before the rapidity disengaged him from his round-house, and even afterwards, such was the impetus, he rolled over several times. To refrain from laughing excessively was impossible, though we really thought the noble fellow must be hurt, when up he jumped, looked round, and said:

"I never had any affection for an empty wine-cask, and may the devil take me if ever I go near another -- to be whirled round like a water-mill in this manner!"

The fellow was in a violent John Bull passion, while we were nearly killed with laughing.

When Massena retired, an order came to the Light Division to move on De Litte, and to Lord Hill to do the same on our right at [Vallada?]. This dispatch I was doomed to carry. It was one of the utmost importance, and required a gallop. By Jove, I had ten miles to go just before dark, and when I got to Colborne's position, who had a Brigade under Lord Hill, a mouse could not get through his works. (Colborne was afterwards my Brigadier in the Light Division, and is now Lord Seaton.) Such a job I never had. I could not go in front of the works -- the French had not retired; so some works I leaped into, and led my noble English horse into others. At last I got to Lord Hill, and he marched immediately, night as it was. How I got back to my Division through the night I hardly know, but horse and rider were both done. The spectacle of hundreds of miserable wretches of French soldiers on the road in a state of starvation is not to be described.

We moved viâ Caccas to Vallé on the [Rio Mayor], where our Division were opposite Santarem. The next day [20 Nov.] the Duke came up and ordered our Division to attack Santarem, which was bristling on our right with abattis, three or four lines. We felt the difficulty of carrying such heights, but towards the afternoon we moved on. On the Duke's staff there was a difference of opinion as to the number of the enemy, whether one corps d armée or two. The Duke, who knew perfectly well there were two, and our move was only a reconnaissance, turned to Colonel Beckwith.

"Beckwith, my Staff are disputing whether at Santarem there is one corps or two?"

"I'll be d—d if I know, my Lord, but you may depend on it, a great number were required to make those abattis in one night."

Lord Wellington laughed, and said, "You are right, Beckwith; there are two corps."

The enemy soon showed themselves. The Duke, as was his wont, satisfied himself by ocular demonstration, and the Division returned to its bivouac. Whilst here, Colonel Beckwith was seized with a violent attack of ague.

Our outposts were perfectly quiet, although sentries, French and English, were at each end of the bridge over the Rio Mayor, and vedettes along each bank. There was most excellent coursing on the plains of Vallé, and James Stewart and I were frequently out. Here I gave him my celebrated Spanish greyhound, Moro, the best the world ever produced, with a pedigree like that of an Arab horse, bred at Zamora by the Conde de Monteron; but the noble dog's story is too long to tell here. In one year Stewart gave me him back again to run a match against the Duke of Wellington's dog. But the siege of Ciudad Rodrigo prevented our sports of that description. Colonel Beckwith going to Lisbon, and I being his A.D.C., it was voted a capital opportunity for me to go to have the ball cut out from under the tendon Achillis, in the very joint. I was very lame, and the pain often excruciating, so off I cut.

Soon after we reached Lisbon, I was ordered to Buenos Ayres to be near the surgeons. A board was held consisting of the celebrated Staff Surgeon Morell, who had attended me before, Higgins, and Brownrigg. They examined my leg. I was all for the operation. Morell and Higgins recommended me to remain with a stiff leg of my own as better than a wooden one, for the wounds in Lisbon of late had sloughed so, they were dubious of the result. Brownrigg said:

"If it were my leg, out should come the ball."

On which I roared out, "Hurrah, Brownrigg, you are the doctor for me."

So Morell says, "Very well, if you are desirous, we will do it directly."

My pluck was somewhat cooled, but I cocked up my leg, and said, "There it is; slash away."

It was five minutes, most painful indeed, before it was extracted. The ball was jagged, and the tendonous fibres had so grown into it, it was half dissected and half torn out, with most excruciating torture for a moment, the forceps breaking which had hold of the ball. George Simmons was present, whose wound had broken out and obliged him to go to Lisbon. The surgeon wanted some linen during the operation, so I said, "George, tear a shirt," which my servant gave him. He turned it about, said, "No, it is a pity; it is a good shirt;" at which I did not — him a few, for my leg was aching and smoking from a wound four or five inches long. Thank God Almighty and a light heart, no sloughing occurred, and before the wound was healed I was with the regiment. Colonel Beckwith's ague was cured, and he had joined his Brigade before I could move, so when I returned to Vallé he was delighted to see his A.D.C.

Chapter 6

Campaign of 1811

I found the army in hourly expectation to move, and the Captain of my Company -- Leach -- was gone sick to the rear, so I said to my Colonel, "I must be no longer A.D.C., sir. However grateful I am, my Company wants me."

"Ah, now you can walk a little, you leave me! Go and be d—d to you; but I love you for the desire."

Off I started, and the very next day we marched [6 Mar. 1811], Massena retreating out of Portugal, and many is the skirmish we had. My leg was so painful, the wound open, and I was so lame. When others could lie down I was on horseback, on a dear little Spanish horse given me by James Stewart, afterwards an animal of still greater renown.

At Pombala I had with my Company a very heavy skirmish [11 Mar.]. At Redinha my Company was in the advance [12 Mar.], supported by Captain O'Hare's. A wood on our front and right was full of Frenchmen. The Light Companies of the 3rd Division came up.

I asked, "Are you going to attack that wood?" A Captain of the 88th Light Company, whom I knew, quite laughed at my question. I said very quietly, "You will be beat back, and when you are, I will move on the edge of the wood and help you." How he laughed! My prediction was very soon verified: he was wounded, and picked up by my Company, which I moved on the right flank of the French and stopped them immediately. I sent to my support, O'Hare, to move up to me. The obstinate old Turk would not, and so I was obliged to come back, and had most unnecessarily five or six men wounded.

The Plain of Redinha is a fine field for military display, and our lines formed to attack Ney's rearguard were magnificent. The enemy had many guns in the field, with prolonged lines, an excellent mode for retreat on such ground, and no rearguard was ever drawn off in more masterly style, while I thought our attack in lines was heavy, slow, and not half so destructive as a rush of many contiguous columns would have been. The enemy had to retire over a bridge through the village of Redinha, and we Riflemen sorely pressed them on their left. A line of French infantry, concealed behind an atalaya (or tower) on a hill good for the purpose, were lying down as my Company and the one commanded by that wonderful Rifleman, Willie Johnstone, got within twenty yards of them. To our astonishment, up jumped the line, fired a volley (they did not hit a man), and went about. At them we all went like devils, a regular foot race, except for me and my little horse Tiny, from which I could not dismount. In the pursuit he carried me down a rock twelve feet high, and Johnstone and I got to the bridge and cut off half a Battalion of French. So many Legions of Honour I scarcely ever saw in a group, but the eagle was off! We never told what we had done, though we enjoyed the fun, but it is an anecdote worthy of record in Napier's History.

We were engaged with the enemy every day. The next turn up was at Condesia [Condeixa]; the next at Casal Nova [14 Mar.], where we had as heavy a skirmishing fight as ever occurred. We Light Division gentlemen had our full complement of fighting, for the French were obliged to hold a village to give their column time to retire, and if the Duke's orders had been obeyed, our Division ought not to have attacked until the 3rd and 4th Divisions were well up on the Frenchmen's left. I lost several men that day, as did all our Companies, and particularly the 52nd. Poor Major Jack Stewart, a dear little fellow, a friend of mine, was shot through the lungs and died in three days, (Beckwith's Brigade Major, Lieut. James Stewart, was in three days [28 Mar., near Freixadas] killed off the very same little English horse, called Tom); Strode, a Lieutenant, received his death-wound while talking to me, etc. That night I was on picquet. The enemy were retiring all night, but their sentries and ours were in sight. At daylight a thick fog came on. Beckwith's Brigade, with him at its head, moved up to where I was posted.

He said, "Come, Harry, get your Company together, and fall in at the head of the column."

At this moment two of the 16th Dragoons rode back, and Beckwith said, "Where do you come from?"

"We have patrolled a league and a half in the front, and seen naught."

"A league and a half, my friend," says old Sydney, "in a thick fog is a d—d long way. Why, Harry, you said the vedettes were close to you."

"So they are," I said, "and you will be fired at the moment you advance." We had not gone fifty yards when "Pop! pop!" Oh, how old Sydney laughed! "A league and a half!" But the fog was so thick we could not move, and the enemy, hearing our column on their rear, being clear, moved off.

In a few days, as we had got well up to the French rear-guard and were about to attack, a General Order was received, to my astonishment, appointing me Brigade Major to the 2nd Light Brigade, not dear old Sydney's. He expected it, since he and Colonel Pakenham were trying to do something for me on account of my lame leg. Beckwith says, "Now give your Company over to Layton, and set off immediately to Colonel Drummond," who commanded the Brigade. Hardly had I reached it, when such a cannonade commenced, knocking the 52nd about in a way I never saw before and hardly since. We were soon all engaged, and drove the French, with very hard fighting, into and over the river, with a severe loss in killed, prisoners, and drowned.

A very heavy fight it was, ending just before dark. I said to my Brigadier, "Have you any orders for the picquets, sir?" He was an old Guardsman, the kindest though oddest fellow possible.

"Pray, Mr. Smith, are you my Brigade Major?"

"I believe so, sir."

"Then let me tell you, it is your duty to post the picquets, and mine to have a d—d good dinner for you every day." We soon understood each other. He cooked the dinner often himself, and I commanded the Brigade.

Our next great fight was a bitter one, Sabugal [3 April]. I shall never forget the German 1st Hussars, my old friends, moving on that day; their singing was melodious. Sir W. Erskine commanded the cavalry and Light Division, a near-sighted old ass, and we got meléed with Reynier's corps strongly posted on heights above Sabugal, and attacked when the Duke intended we should have moved round their left to Quadraseyes, as the 5th, 4th, and 3rd Divisions were to attack their front in the centre of their position. However, we began, and never was more gallantry mutually displayed by friend and foe than on this occasion, particularly by dear old Beckwith and his 1st Brigade. Some guns were taken and retaken several times. A French officer on a grey horse was most gallant.

Old Beckwith, in a voice like thunder, roared out to the Riflemen, "Shoot that fellow, will you?" In a moment he and his horse were knocked over, and Sydney exclaimed, "Alas! you were a noble fellow."

My Brigadier, as I soon discovered, left the command to me, so I led away, and we came in for a pretty good share in preventing Reynier's turning the left of Beckwith's Brigade. Fortunately, the 5th Division got into action just in time, for the French at the moment were squeezing us awfully. The Light Division, under the shout of old Beckwith, rushed on with an impetuosity nothing could resist, for, so checked had we been, our bloods were really up, and we paid off the enemy most awfully. Such a scene of slaughter as there was on one hill would appal a modern soldier. The night came on most awfully wet, and the 5th and Light Division were sent back to Sabugal for shelter. Most dilapidated the place was, but the roofs were on, and Sir W. Gomm, A.Q.M.G. of the 5th, and I divided the town between us, our poor wounded lying out in the rain and cold all night. The next morning was fine, and as the sun rose we marched over the field of battle. Our soldiers' blood was then cool, and it was beautiful to hear the remarks of sympathy for the distress of the numerous dying and wounded all around us. Oh, you kings and usurpers should view these scenes and moderate ambition!

This evening [4 April] we had a long march into Quadraseyes, but did not see a vestige of the enemy all day, nor of our commissariat either. We were literally starving. That old rogue Picton had seized the supplies of the Light Division for his 3rd. If he be now in the Purgatory that we condemned him to, he is to be pitied.

We closely pursued the French over the frontier, but never had a real slap at them. Almeida, which was garrisoned by their troops, was invested by the 5th Division, while the Light Division moved into its old lines, Gallegos, Marialva, Carpio, and Espeja. From the French garrison of Ciudad Rodrigo the enemy frequently came out. The Duke had gone into the Alemtejo, and Sir Brent Spencer commanded -- a regular old woman, who allowed the French to commit all sorts of extravagances under our noses, when a rapid move on their rear from Espeja would have punished them. Sir W. Erskine commanded the advance Cavalry and Light Division.

I was at breakfast one morning with Sir William Erskine, who, early in the morning, with his staff had taken out a small party to reconnoitre Ciudad Rodrigo. The enemy immediately sent over a detachment of cavalry to check the advance, and a great argument occurred between Sir William and his A.A.G., Macdonald, whether the enemy crossed one or two squadrons. During the discussion in came Sir William's orderly, a clever old dragoon of the 1st German Hussars.

"Ah!" says Sir William, "here is my old orderly; he can tell us. Hussar, how many squadrons of the enemy crossed the Agueda this morning?"

With a body as stiff and erect as a statue, and a salute with an arm braced as if in the act of cutting down his enemy, "Just forty-nine mans, no more; I count him."

The laugh was against both disputants.

Now occurred the dreadful disaster of the escape of the French garrison of Almeida. I shall never forget the mortification of our soldiers or the admiration of our officers of the brilliancy of such an attempt, the odds being a hundred to one against success. My long friend Ironmonger, then of the Queen's, into whose face George Simmons threw the bucket of water when marching, as before described, from Belem, was grievously to blame.

Massena's army were rapidly recovering. They had received re-inforcements, and were preparing to throw into Ciudad Rodrigo a large convoy of provisions. For this, it was necessary for them to put us back, and the present moment seemed a favourable one, as it was the intention ultimately to withdraw the French army to

Salamanca and the neighbouring large towns, so that no demand might be made on the ample supplies required for Ciudad Rodrigo. At this moment Soult was making a formidable demonstration in the Alemtejo and Estremadura, our attempt on Badajoz had failed, and a large portion of our army had moved towards the south; it was therefore a fair opening for Massena to drive us over the Coa.

However, the dear Duke of Wellington took a braver view of the situation, and concentrated his army behind Fuentes D'Oñoro, and there fought that celebrated battle which lasted a day and a half [5 May]. General Craufurd joined us here on the day of the general action. The soldiers received him with every demonstration of joy. The officers at that time execrated him. I did not; he had appointed me his A.D.C., though I would not go to him, and he was always most kind and hospitable to me.

On the morning of this day old Sydney again distinguished himself, for the enemy from Poza Velha turned our right flank and licked our cavalry (14th Light Dragoons and Royals) awfully, bringing 4000 fresh fellows against them. There never was a more heavy fight than for several hours in the village of Fuentes. Here I saw the 79th Regiment, in an attack on the head of a French column coming up the road, bayonet eight or nine French officers and upwards of 100 men, the only real bayonet conflict I ever witnessed. After the battle of Fuentes d'Oñoro, the French retired unmolested, for we were glad to get rid of them. As they had such a formidable body of cavalry, on that open country we literally could not molest them.

At this time almost all our army moved into the Alemtejo viá Arronchas, where, on Sir John Moore's advance to Salamanca, I had a nice quarter which I occupied four different times during the war. The poor family were always delighted to see me. On our advance into the Alemtejo we heard of the bloody battle of Albuera [16 May], and many of us rode on to see the field, which was well demonstrated by the lines of dead bodies, a most sanguinary conflict, and beautifully and truly described by Napier.

I must here record a most ridiculous night alarm the Light Division had, although leagues from any enemy, on their march into the Alemtejo. A drove of bullocks galloped over our men asleep in the bivouac, and for some time the officers could hardly persuade our best soldiers they were not French cavalry. My Brigadier, Drummond, was sleeping under a tree on his little portable iron bedstead. The light of a fire showed him, to my amusement, in his shirt (not a very long one), endeavouring to climb into the tree. I fell in his guard, and manfully charged nothing up a road leading to our camp, while General Craufurd lay on his back laughing to hysterics, poor fellow. Drummond soon after died at Guinaldo, in my arms, of a putrid sore throat, and Craufurd was killed in the storm of Ciudad Rodrigo.

During all this summer our army was assembled watching Soult, who neither attacked us nor we him. Never did we spend a more inactive summer. The enemy from Ciudad Rodrigo moved on Castello Branco, and threatened thereby our left flank and line of communication over the Tagus. When Soult could no longer feed his assembled army, he retired, and our Light Division were rapidly moved on Castello Branco, the remainder of the army of the north following.

Our army this autumn was cantoned, as near as it could be fed, on the frontiers to watch Ciudad Rodrigo, which the Duke contemplated besieging. After the death of General Drummond, Major-General Vandeleur was appointed to my Brigade, a fine, gentleman-like old Irish hero. We were quartered at Martiago, and our Division, some at El Bodon, others at Zamora, Guinaldo, etc. It was a very hot autumn, but towards the end of the year, when the rains commenced, there was capital coursing.

General Craufurd this year, in one of his mad freaks, reported that the Light Division was in want of clothing, etc., and it must go to the rear. The Duke ordered us to march one cold night over the Agueda to Larade, not far from Guinaldo, for his inspection. A great scene occurred. Craufurd had not arrived before the Duke rode down the line, and the Duke laughed and said:

"Craufurd, you are late."

"No, my Lord; you are before your time. My watch is to be depended on."

I was riding a brown mare which I gave £120 for to Charlie Rowan, who had been thrown by her, after buying her from General Craufurd because he could not ride her. The mare charged the Duke, I on her back.

"Hallo, Smith," says the Duke, "your horse masters you." The Duke, to our delight, says to General Craufurd, "I never saw the Light Division look better or more ready for service. March back to your quarters; I shall soon require you in the field."

About this time Marmont moved up to Ciudad Rodrigo with an enormous convoy of provisions and he compelled the Duke to assemble, and the brilliant affair of cavalry and squares of infantry behind El Bodon took place [24 Sept.].

About this time we had some heavy and laborious manoeuvring, night marches, etc. During these movements we marched a dark night's march from Guinaldo, and, as the road was wet and far from good, we had several checks in the column, when I heard a conversation between a 16th Light Dragoon and one of the German 1st Hussars, neither of whom had abstained from the ingredient which formed the subject. 16th Dragoon:

"I say, Hussar, I likes it strong and hot and sweet, and plenty of —. How do you like it?"

Hussar: "I likes him raw."

Marmont, having accomplished his object, fell back, and we returned to our old cantonments. The Duke of Wellington's dispatch dated "Quadrasies, Sept. 29," so fully details all these operations and shows the beauty of the manoeuvres so distinctly, I may confine myself to what occurred the evening General Pakenham's brigade had such a formidable brush at Aldea de Ponte.

The 4th Division was to return at dusk, as was the Light. I was lying in bivouac, talking to General Craufurd and John Bell, when a dragoon rode up with a note from General Cole, requesting Craufurd to send an officer as a guide to lead his division to the heights of Rendo at dusk.

I said, "Oh, John Bell will go, of course."

"No," says John; "Harry Smith knows the road best."

So I was ordered to go. Before I reached Cole it was dark. I found his Division moving: they were all right. I reported myself to him -- the first time I had ever spoken to him. Colonel Brooke, brother of the "Shannon" Brooke, his Q.M.G., was with him.

"Oh," says Cole, "sent by Craufurd, are you? Do you know the road?"

We Light Division gentlemen were proper saucy fellows. I said, "I suppose I should not have been sent if I had not."

"Ugh," says Cole, as hot as pepper.

Here I may remark upon the difficulty there is at night to know roads, even for one well acquainted with them. Fires lighting, fires going out, the covering of the country with troops -- such things change the face of nature, and a little anxiety adds to the difficulty. Cole, a most anxious man, kept saying:

"Are you sure you know the road, sir?" etc, etc, etc.

At last I said, "General Cole, if you will let me alone, I will conduct your Division; if you thus attract my attention, I cannot."

It was an anxious moment, I admit. I was just at a spot where I might miss the road, a great road which I knew was near. I galloped ahead to look for it, and oh, how General Cole did blow me up!

I found my road, though, and so soon as the head of the column had fairly reached it, I said, "Good night, General," and in a moment was in full speed, while he was hallooing to me to come back.

I had some difficulty in finding my own Division, which was moving parallel with the force. When I told Craufurd of my first acquaintance with that hot Irishman Cole, how he laughed! On one of our marches from the Alemtejo to the north, in a house where General Drummond and I were quartered at Idanha a Nova, a very facetious Portuguese gentleman showed us a sort of a return of the British, so incorrect that General Drummond laughed at it; but Charlie Rowan, our A.A.G., who was dining with General Drummond, told this anecdote at the Duke's table at Guinaldo, and I was sent back about 150 miles to fetch my friend. I could speak Portuguese as well as English. I therefore persuaded our hero to accompany me to the Duke without telling why, but a more unpleasant ride than this, in charge of my friend and all alone, without groom, etc., I never had, and many was the blessing

I bestowed on Charlie Rowan's tongue. I delivered my friend to the Adjutant-General at Guinaldo, and had twenty-four miles to join my General at Robledillo.

Chapter 7

Campaign of 1812 -- Storming of Ciudad Rodrigo

As the winter approached we had private theatricals. The Duke appointed so many days for horse races, greyhound matches, etc., and the very day they were to come off, which was well known to the French army, we invested Ciudad Rodrigo, namely, on the 8th of January, 1812, and that very night carried by storm the outworks called Fort San Francisco, up to which spot it took the French several days to approach. We broke ground, and thus the siege commenced.

When the detachments of the Light Division Brigades were parading, my Brigade was to furnish 400 men. I understood four Companies, and when Colonel Colborne (now Lord Seaton) was counting them, he said:

"There are not the complement of men." I said, "I am sorry if I have mistaken."

"Oh, never mind; run and bring another Company."

I mention this to show what a cool, noble fellow he is. Many an officer would have stormed like fury. He only thought of storming Fort San Francisco, which he carried in a glorious manner.

The siege was carried on by four Divisions -- 1st, 3rd, 4th, and Light, cantoned as near Ciudad Rodrigo as possible. One Division was on duty at a time, and each had to ford the Agueda the day it was for duty. The Light was at El Bodon. We had a distance of nine miles to march every fourth day, and back on the fifth, so that we had only three days' halt. The frost was excessive, and there was some little snow, but fortunately the weather was fine above head.

The Light Division stormed the little breach on the evening of the 19th of January (nine o' clock). I was supping with my dear friend Captain Uniacke, and brother Tom, his only subaltern not wounded. When I parted from Uniacke -- he was a noble, light-hearted fellow -- he says:

"Harry, you will be a Captain before morning."

Little, poor fellow, did he think he was to make the vacancy. I was senior subaltern of the 95th, and I went to General Craufurd and volunteered the forlorn hope that was given to Gurwood. Craufurd said:

"Why, you cannot go; you, a Major of Brigade, a senior Lieutenant, you are sure to get a Company. No, I must give it to a younger officer." This was to me a laborious night. Just as my Brigade had to march, I discovered the Engineer officer had not brought up the ladders, fascines, and bundles of hay, and old George Simmons was sent for them.

In ascending the breach, I got on a ravelin at the head of the 43rd and 52nd, moving in column together. Colborne pulled me down again, and up the right breach we ascended. I saw the great breach, stormed by the 3rd Division, was ably defended, and a line behind a work which, as soon as we rushed along the ramparts, we could enfilade. I seized a Company of the 43rd and rushed on the flank, and opened a fire which destroyed every man behind the works. My conduct caused great annoyance to the Captain, Duffy, with whom I had some very high words; but the Company obeyed me, and then ran on with poor Uniacke's Company to meet the 3rd Division, or rather clear the ramparts to aid them, when the horrid explosion took place which killed General Mackinnon of the 3rd division on the spot and many soldiers, awfully scorching others. I and Uniacke were much scorched, but some splinters of an ammunition chest lacerated him and caused his death three days after the storm. Tom, my brother, was not hurt.

I shall never forget the concussion when it struck me, throwing me back many feet into a lot of charged fuses of shells, which in the confusion I took for shells. But a gallant fellow, a Sergeant MacCurrie, 52nd Regiment, soon put me right, and prevented me leaping into the ditch. My cocked hat was blown away, my clothes all singed; however the sergeant, a noble fellow, lent me a catskin forage-cap, and on we rushed to meet the 3rd Division, which we soon did. It was headed by a great, big thundering Grenadier of the 88th, a Lieutenant Stewart, and one of his men seized me by the throat as if I were a kitten, crying out, "You

French —." Luckily, he left me room in the windpipe to d— his eyes, or the bayonet would have been through me in a moment.

Gurwood got great credit here unfairly. Willie Johnstone and poor Uniacke were the two first on the ramparts, Gurwood having been knocked down in the breach and momentarily stunned, which enabled them to get before him. However, Gurwood's a sharp fellow, and he cut off in search of the Governor, and brought his sword to the Duke, and Lord Fitzroy Somerset buckled it on him in the breach. Gurwood made the most of it.

We had many officers of rank wounded. George Napier, of the 52nd, lost an arm; the General of Brigade, Vandeleur, was wounded severely in the shoulder; and Colonel Colborne, of the 52nd, received an awful wound, but he never quitted his Regiment until the city was perfectly ours, and his Regiment all collected. A musket-ball had struck him under the epaulette of his right shoulder, and broken the head of the bone right off in the socket. To this the attention of the surgeons was of course directed. Some months after Colborne complained of a pain four inches below where the ball entered, and suppuration took place, and by surgical treatment the bone was gradually exposed. The ball, after breaking the arm above, had descended and broken the arm four inches below, and was firmly embedded in the bone. The pain he suffered in the extraction of the ball was more even than his iron heart could bear. He used to lay his watch on the table and allow the surgeons five minutes' exertions at a time, and they were three or four days before they wrenched the ball from its ossified bed. In three weeks from that day Colborne was in the Pyrenees, and in command of his Regiment. Of course the shoulder joint was anchylosed, but he had free use of the arm below the elbow.

After this siege we had a few weeks' holiday, with the exception of shooting some rascals who had deserted to the enemy. Eleven knelt on one grave at Ituero. It is an awful ceremony, a military execution. I was Major of Brigade of the day. The Provost-Marshal had not told the firing off, so that a certain number of men should shoot one culprit, and so on, but at his signal the whole party fired a volley. Some prisoners were fortunate enough to be killed, others were only wounded, some untouched. I galloped up. An unfortunate Rifleman called to me by name -- he was awfully wounded -- "Oh, Mr. Smith, put me out of my misery," and I literally ordered the firing party, when reloaded, to run up and shoot the poor wretches. It was an awful scene.

"Blood he had viewed, but then
it flowed in combat..."

Chapter 8

Campaign of 1812 -- The Storming of Badajos -- Harry Smith's Marriage

At this period of the year (February, March) the coursing in this part of Spain is capital, and by help of my celebrated dog Moro and two other excellent ones, I supplied the officers' mess of every Company with hares for soup We had a short repose, for the army moved into Estremadura for the purpose of besieging Badajos. We Light, 3rd and 4th Divisions, thought, as we had taken Ciudad Rodrigo, others would have the pleasure of the trenches of Badajos, but on our reaching Elvas [17 Feb., 1812] we were very soon undeceived, and we were destined for the duty, -- to our mortification, for soldiers hate sieges and working-parties. The Guards work better than any soldiers, from their habits in London. Badajos was invested by the 3rd, 4th, and Light Divisions on the Spanish side, or left bank of the river, and by the 5th Division, on the Portuguese side, or right bank. On the night of the 17th March, St. Patrick's Day, the Light Division broke ground under a deluge of rain, which swelled the Guadiana so as to threaten our bridge of boats. Our duties in the trenches were most laborious during the whole siege, and much hard fighting we had, sorties, etc. The night [26 Mar.] the out-works La Picurina was carried by my dear friend Sir James Kempt, part of the 3rd Division (which was his) were to compose the storming party. The Light Division, the working party, consequently were sent to the Engineer Park for the ladders. When they arrived, General Kempt ordered them to be planted (Sir H. Hardinge, D.Q.M.G. of the Portuguese army, was here distinguished). The boys of the 3rd Division said to our fellows:

"Come, stand out of the way."

To which our fellows replied, "D— your eyes, do you think we Light Division fetch ladders for such chaps as you to climb up? Follow us" -- springing on the ladders, and many of them were knocked over.

A notorious fellow, a Sergeant Brotherwood, a noble fellow

on duty, told me this anecdote. The siege was prosecuted with the same vigour from without with which it was repelled from within.

After some hours in the trenches, when we returned I invariably ate and went out coursing, and many is the gallant course I had, and many the swift hare I and my dog Moro brought home from the right bank of the Guadiana. One day James Stewart, I, and Charlie Eeles set off; having three hours off duty, to look for a hare or two at a celebrated spot where the hares ran very strong because there was a rabbit warren which saved them. Moro, of course, was of the party. We soon found an unusually strong hare, and, although the greyhounds fetched round a dozen times, she still worked her way for the warren. I was riding a great stupid Irish horse bought from General Vandeleur, called Paddy, and as it was important for the soup to kill this hare, however unsportsmanlike on quiet occasions it would be deemed, I rode to head her from the warren. My stupid beast of a horse put his foot into a hole and rolled over me. Stewart and Eeles picked me up, but I was insensible. Although I have generally managed on such occasions to get away from the horse, the animal had rolled over me, and when I came to myself I was sitting on Eeles' knee, my arms tied up with a whip-thong, and James Stewart, with a blunt-looking penknife, trying to bleed me, an operation I quickly prohibited by starting on to my legs. Moro killed his hare, though, without my help.

On the night of the 6th April the 3rd Division were to storm the citadel, the 4th and Light the great breach, the 5th the Olivença Gate, and to escalade, if possible. The command of the Light Division had devolved on Colonel Barnard. Vandeleur was wounded, and stayed at Portalegre, and poor Beckwith had gone to the rear with violent ague; he never joined us again, noble soldier that he was.

This escalade has been so frequently described, I shall only say that when the head of the Light Division arrived at the ditch of the place it was a beautiful moonlight night. Old Alister Cameron, who was in command of four Companies of the 95th Regiment, extended along the counterscape to attract the enemy's fire, while the column planted their ladders and descended, came up to Barnard and said:

"Now my men are ready; shall I begin?"

"No, certainly not," says Barnard. The breach and the works were full of the enemy, looking quietly at us, but not fifty yards off and most prepared, although not firing a shot. So soon as our ladders were all ready posted, and the column in the very act to move and rush down the ladders, Barnard called out, "Now, Cameron!" and the first shot from us brought down such a hail of fire as I shall never forget, nor ever saw before or since. It was most murderous.

We flew down the ladders and rushed at the breach, but we were broken, and carried no weight with us, although every soldier was a hero. The breach was covered by a breastwork from behind, and ably defended on the top by chevaux-de-frises of sword-blades, sharp as razors, chained to the ground; while the ascent to the top of the breach was covered with planks with sharp nails in them. However, devil a one did I feel at this moment. One of the officers of the forlorn hope, Lieut. Taggart of the 43rd, was hanging on my arm -- a mode we adopted to help each other up, for the ascent was most difficult and steep. A Rifleman stood among the sword-blades on the top of one of the chevaux-de-frises. We made a glorious rush to follow, but, alas! in vain. He was knocked over. My old captain, O'Hare, who commanded the storming party, was killed. All were awfully wounded except, I do believe, myself and little Freer of the 43rd.

I had been some seconds at the revêtement of the bastion near the breach, and my red-coat pockets were literally filled with chips of stones splintered by musket-balls. Those not knocked down were driven back by this hail of mortality to the ladders. At the foot of them I saw poor Colonel Macleod with his hands on his breast -- the man who lent me his horse when wounded at the bridge on the Coa.

He said, "Oh, Smith, I am mortally wounded. Help me up the ladder."

I said, "Oh no, dear fellow!"

"I am," he said; "be quick!" I did so, and came back again. Little Freer and I said:

"Let us throw down the ladders; the fellows shan't go out."

Some soldiers behind said, "D— your eyes, if you do we will bayonet you!" and we were literally forced up with the crowd.

My sash had got loose, and one end of it was fast in the ladder, and the bayonet was very nearly applied, but the sash by pulling became loose. So soon as we got on the glacis, up came a fresh Brigade of the Portuguese of the 4th Division. I never saw any soldiers behave with more pluck. Down into the ditch we all went again, but the more we tried to get up, the more we were destroyed. The 4th Division followed us in marching up to the breach, and they made a most uncommon noise. The French saw us, but took no notice. Sir Charles Colville, commanding the 4th Division (Cole having been wounded at Albuera), made a devil of a noise, too, on the glacis. Both Divisions were fairly beaten back; we never carried either breach (nominally there were two breaches).

After the attacks upon the breaches, some time before daylight Lord Fitzroy Somerset came to our Division. I think I was almost the first officer who spoke to him.

He said, "Where is Barnard?" I didn't know, but I assured his Lordship he was neither killed nor wounded. A few minutes after his Lordship said that the Duke desired the Light and 4th Divisions to storm again.

"The devil!" says I. "Why, we have had enough; we are all knocked to pieces."

Lord Fitzroy says, "I dare say, but you must try again."

I smiled and said, "If we could not succeed with two whole fresh and unscathed Divisions, we are likely to make a poor show of it now. But we will try again with all our might."

Scarcely had this conversation occurred when a bugle sounded within the breach, indicating what had occurred at the citadel and the Puerto de Olivença; and here ended all the fighting. Our fellows would have gone at it again when collected and put into shape, but we were just as well pleased that our attempt had so attracted the attention of the enemy as greatly to facilitate that success which assured the prize contended for.

There is no battle, day or night, I would not willingly react except this. The murder of our gallant officers and soldiers is not to be believed. Next day I and Charlie Beckwith, a brother Brigade-Major, went over the scene. It was appalling. Heaps on heaps of slain, -- in one spot lay nine officers. Whilst we were there, Colonel Allen of the Guards came up, and beckoned me to him. I saw that, in place of congratulating me, he looked very dull.

"What's the matter?" I said. "Do you not know my brother in the Rifles was killed last night?"

"God help him and you! no, for I and we all loved him." In a flood of tears, he looked round and pointed to a body. "There he lies." He had a pair of scissors with him. "Go and cut off a lock of his hair for my mother. I came for the purpose, but I am not equal to doing it."

The returns of killed and wounded and the evident thin appearance of our camp at once too plainly told the loss we had sustained. O memorable night of glory and woe! for, although the 4th and Light were so beaten, our brilliant and numerous attacks induced the governor to concentrate all his force in the breaches; thus the 3rd escaladed the citadel, and the 5th got in by the Olivença gate. Although we lost so many stout hearts, so many dear friends and comrades, yet not one staff officer of our Division was killed or wounded. We had all been struck. My clothes were cut by musket-balls, and I had several contusions, particularly one on my left thigh.

Now comes a scene of horror I would willingly bury in oblivion. The atrocities committed by our soldiers on the poor innocent and defenceless inhabitants of the city, no words suffice to depict. Civilized man, when let loose and the bonds of morality relaxed, is a far greater beast than the savage, more refined in his cruelty, more fiend-like in every act; and oh, too truly did our heretofore noble soldiers disgrace themselves, though the officers exerted themselves to the utmost to repress it, many who had escaped the enemy being wounded in their merciful attempts! Yet this scene of debauchery, however cruel to many, to me has been the solace and the whole happiness of my life for thirty-three years.

After the disorganization our troops had rushed into, it became the duty of every officer to exert himself, and nobly did Colonel Barnard set about the task, and ably supported was he by every officer in the Division. We had not marched for the north two days when our soldiers were, like Richard, "themselves again." When the French garrison were marched to the rear, my Brigade furnished an escort to the next Division en route to Elvas. I paraded upwards of four thousand very orderly, fine-looking fellows. Many of the officers praised the gallantry of our men, and all said, "Why break ground at all with such soldiers? Had you stormed on the rainy night of the 17th March, you would have taken the place with half the loss." This is creditable to us, but the Duke of Wellington would have been by no means borne out in such an attempt.

However, as all this writing is to show rather my individual participation in these scenes of glory and bloodshed, I must dwell a little upon the joy of my marriage. I was only twenty-two, my wife just on the verge of fourteen. But in southern climates Nature more early develops herself and attains maturity. Every day was an increase of joy. Although both of us were of the quickest tempers, we were both ready to forgive, and both intoxicated in happiness. All my dearest friends -- Charlie Beckwith, John Bell, Johnstone, Charlie Eeles, Jack Molloy, etc. -- were saying to themselves, "Alas! poor Harry Smith is lost, who was the example of a duty-officer previously. It is only natural he must neglect duty now."

I assured them all that the contrary would be the case, for love would incite me to exertions in hopes of preferment, the only mode I had to look to for a comfortable maintenance; and my wife's love, aided by her good sense, would see I was never neglecting her if engaged in the performance of my duty. Conscientiously did I act up to my feeling then, and no one ever did or ever could say, I was out of my place night or day.

My duty was my duty -- I gloried in it; my wife even still more so, and never did she say, "You might have been with me," or complain if I was away. On the contrary, after many a day's fatiguing march, when I sought her out in the baggage or awaiting me, her first question invariably was, "Are you sure you have done all your duty?" Then I admit my attention was unbounded, and we were happy -- oh, how happy, often amidst scenes of distress and privation that would have appalled stouter hearts, not devoted like ours!

Chapter 9

Campaign of 1812 -- Battle of Salamanca -- Occupation of Madrid -- Retreat to Salamanca

Hardly had we reached the frontier of Portugal [24 April, 1812], our old haunts, Ituero, Guinaldo, etc., when our army moved on again for Spain, and fought the Battle of Salamanca. Before this battle we had an immense deal of marching and manoeuvring. The armies of Marmont and Wellington were close to each other for several days, so that a trifling occurrence would have brought on a general action, and we were frequently under cannonade.

My wife could not ride in the least at first, although she had frequently ridden a donkey on her pilgrimage to Olivença, once to avoid the siege of Badajos, and at other times to her grandmother's at Almendrajos. However, I had one of my saddles turned into a side-saddle most ably by a soldier of Ross's Troop of Horse Artillery, and at first made her ride a great brute of a Portuguese horse I had; but she so rapidly improved, took such pains, had so much practice and naturally good nerves, that she soon got ashamed of her Portuguese horse, and wanted to ride my Spanish little fellow, who had so nobly carried me at Redinha and in many other fights. I always said, "When you can ride as well as you can dance and sing, you shall," for in those accomplishments she was perfect.

In crossing the Tormes [21 July], the very night before the battle of Salamanca (there are quicksands in the river), her Portuguese horse was so cowardly he alarmed me, and hardly had we crossed the river when a clap of thunder, louder than anything that can be described, burst over our heads. The Portuguese horse was in such a funk, she abjured all Portuguese, and insisted hereafter on riding her own gallant countryman, as gallant as any Arab. He was an Andalusian, which is a thorough-bred descendant of the Moosul horse, which is literally an Arab. The next day she mounted her Tiny, and rode him ever afterwards over many an eventful field, until the end of the war at Toulouse. She had him afterwards at my father's house. The affection between them was of the character of that between spaniel and master. The dear, gallant horse lived to twenty-nine years of age, and died a happy pensioner on my brother Charles's estate.

It is difficult to say who was the proudest on the morning of the battle [22 July], horse, wife, or Enrique (as I was always called). She caracoled him about among the soldiers, to their delight, for he was broken in like a Mameluke, though very difficult to ride. (The soldiers of the whole Division loved her with enthusiasm from the events so peculiar in her history, and she would laugh and talk with all, which a soldier loves. Blackguards as many of the poor gallant fellows were, there was not a man who would not have laid down his life to defend her, and among the officers she was adored, and consulted on all occasions of baggage-guard, etc.) Her attendant, who also had a led horse in case of accident, with a little tent and a funny little pair of lanterns, my dear, trusty old groom West, as the battle began, took her to the rear, much to her annoyance, and in the thunder of cannon, the pride of equestrianism was buried in anxiety for him on whom her all depended. She and West slept on the field of battle, he having made a bed for her with the green wheat he had cut just in full ear. She had to hold her horse all night, and he ate all her bed of green wheat, to her juvenile amusement; for a creature so gay and vivacious, with all her sound sense, the earth never produced.

Next morning soon after daylight she joined me on the march. I was at that time so afflicted with boils, I could hardly live on horseback. I had eleven immense ones at the time on my legs and thighs, the excruciating pain of which is not to be described. Our surgeon, old Joe Bowker, insisted on my going to Salamanca, and one particular boil on the bone of the inside of my knee proved a more irresistible argument. So to Salamanca I had to go, my brother Tom doing my duty. I stayed fourteen days at Salamanca, a time of love and excitement, although, so distressed was the army for money, we lived almost on our rations, except for a little assistance from the lady of our house in coffee, etc. Wade, Sir Lowry Cole's A.D.C., lent me one dollar out of forty which he had received to support his General (who had been severely wounded in the battle), and his staff. In such times of privation heroism is required which our countrymen little dream of.

At the end of the fourteen days I had as many boils as ever, but, boils and all, off we started, and rode some terrible distances for three or four days. We overtook the Division, to the joy of the soldiers, before we crossed the Guadarama Pass [11 Aug.] There had been no fighting in my absence, thank God.

We soon reached the neighbourhood of Madrid. No city could be better laid out for pomp and show, and the Duke's entry [13 Aug.] was a most brilliant spectacle. My vivacious wife used to enjoy her native capital, and in her admiration treated London and Paris as villages in comparison. We spent a very happy time. It was a great amusement to improve our wardrobe for the walk on the elegant Prado of an evening, in which no love among the Spanish beauties showed to greater advantage than my Estremenha, or native of Estremadura. During our stay in the vicinity of Madrid we made several agreeable acquaintances, among others the vicar of one of the many rich villages around Madrid, Vicalbaro, a highly educated and clever fellow, a great sportsman and excellent shot, with a morbid hatred to a Frenchman.

Upon our moving forward beyond Madrid as far as the beautiful and clean city Alcala [23 Oct.], I was brought in contact with the celebrated and unfortunate General Elio, whom I had known in South America at Monte Video. He was very conversational, and we had a long talk as to that colonial war; but, as I was acting as interpreter for my friend James Stewart, the A.Q.M.G. of our Division, who was making arrangements of march with Elio, conversation on the past turned into plans for the future. We moved forwards towards our right to Arganda [27 Oct.]. At this period the Duke had gone to Burgos, and Lord Hill commanded.

We soon felt the loss of our decided and far-seeing chief, and we made marches and counter-marches we were unaccustomed to. At ten at night, at Arganda, Major-General Vandeleur received an order from General Alten, who remained in Alcala, to march immediately back to Alcala with the whole Division. Vandeleur sent for me and told me to order the assembly to sound. I remonstrated and prayed him to wait until two hours before daylight, for every soldier in the Division had more or less indulged in the wine for which Arganda was celebrated. The good general had been at the shrine of Bacchus too, and was uncontrollable. Blast went the assembly, and staggering to their alarm-posts went the soldiers. Such a scene of good-natured riot I had never seen in my own Division. With the Duke we generally had a sort of hint we might be wanted, and our tried soldiers would be as steady as rocks. Oh, such a dark night's march as we had back to Alcala! Vandeleur repented of his obstinacy, and well he might.

We halted the next day at Alcala. Here, although it was now October, it was evident to me that a long retreat to the frontier was about to be undertaken, and I got from a Spanish officer, called Labrador, his fine large Andalusian horse in exchange for an Irish brute I had bought from General Vandeleur. He gave me three Spanish doubloons to boot, a fortune in those days, particularly to me.

These three doubloons were given to my vivacious Spanish wife, who put them up most carefully in my portmanteau, among my few shirts. On the march the motion of the mule had shaken them out of place, the doubloons were gone, and all our fortune! Her horror, poor girl, is not to be described. She knew it was our all, and her delight when I gave the treasure into her charge was now more than eclipsed by the misery of the loss. I only laughed, for in those days hardships and privations were so common, they were missed when comparative affluence supplied their place.

We marched [30 Oct.] to Madrid, or rather its suburbs, where the poor inhabitants were in indescribable distress, seeing that they were again to be abandoned to French clemency and contributions. While our troops were halted, waiting for orders whether to bivouac or whether to retire, to our astonishment up came the Vicar of Vicalbaro. He took me on one side, and told me most pathetically that he had made himself so obnoxious to the French, he feared to stay, and had come to crave my protection. This I gladly promised. While I described to him the hardships a winter retreat would impose upon him and us, he said gallantly,:

"I am young and healthy like yourselves; what you suffer, I can. My only fear is that I may inconvenience you and my young countrywoman, your wife."

I laughed, and called her. She was all fun, notwithstanding the loss of the doubloons, and began to quiz him; but in the midst of her raillery he observed, as he said to me afterwards, her soul of kindness, and the Padre was installed in my establishment, while my old comrades laughed and said, "Harry Smith will do, now he has a father confessor," by which name the Padre always went -- "Harry Smith's confessor." The hour or two of halt was occupied by the padre in buying a pony which he soon effected, and his marching establishment, a few shirts, with an immense capa, or cloak, almost as much as the pony could carry.

It rained in torrents, and we marched to Aravaca, some miles to the rear of the capital, where we found Lord Hill's headquarters in possession of every hole in the village, which was a very small one. General Vandeleur, who was still suffering from his wound at Ciudad Rodrigo, found a Captain of the Waggon Train in possession of a small house. In walks the General to a nice clean little room with a cheerful fire.

"Who are you, sir?" says the General.

"I am Captain —, of the Royal Waggon Train, attached to Lord Hill, and this house is given me for my quarters."

"I, sir, am General Vandeleur, and am d—d glad to see you in my quarters for five minutes."

The poor Captain very quietly packed up his traps and went -- I know not where.

I, my young wife, the Padre, all my greyhounds and dogs, about thirteen, got into a little hole about six feet square, and were glad enough to get out of the rain, for, though my wife had her little tent, that, pitched on exceedingly wet ground, was a horrid shelter for any one. Owing to the kindness of our Provost-Marshal (Mr. Stanway), I got my horses also under a kind of out-office. We marched the next day to the foot of the Guadarama Pass, where our soldiers, when dismissed in bivouac, had a fine hunt after a wild boar, which they killed. The sunshine brightened, and when I returned from a variety of duties I found the young wife as neat as a new pin in her little tent, her habit and all her things which had got wet in yesterday's rain hung out to dry. So after breakfast I proposed to decorate my person (shave I need not, for as yet that operation was unnecessary), and the portmanteau was opened, the delinquent from which our doubloons had escaped. Some of the shirts were wet from the rain, and in searching for a dry one, out tumbled the three doubloons, which had been shaken into the folds of the shirt by the motion of the mule, and so lost. Oh, such joy and such laughing! We were so rich. We could buy bread and chocolate and sausages and eggs through the interest of the Padre (for we found the holy friar could get things when, however much money was exhibited, it proved no talisman), and our little fortune carried us through the retreat even to Ciudad Rodrigo, where money was paid to us.

This retreat was a very severe one as to weather, and although the enemy did not actually press us, as he did the column from Burgos, we made long marches and were very broad awake, and lost some of our baggage and stores, which the wearied bullocks obliged us to abandon. On reaching Salamanca, my wife, with the foresight of age rather than youth, expended some of the doubloons in buying me two pairs of worsted stockings and a pair of worsted mits, and the same for herself; which I do believe saved her from sickness, for the rain, on the retreat from Salamanca, came in torrents.

Chapter 10

Campaign of 1812 -- Retreat to the lines of Torres Vedras -- Winter of 1812-13

The army concentrated again under the dear Duke of Wellington, and took up its old victorious position on the Arapiles [14 Nov.], but not with the same prospects. Soult, an able fellow, had nearly double our force, and so soon as our rear was open the army was in full march on Ciudad Rodrigo. It rained in torrents, and the roads rose above the soldiers' ankles. Our supplies were nil and the sufferings of the soldiers were considerable. Many compared this retreat with that of Coruña, at which I then laughed, and do now. The whole distance from Ciudad Rodrigo is only forty-four miles. On one day to Coruña we marched thirty-seven miles, fighting every yard, and the cold was intense; on this retreat it was cold, but no frost in the atmosphere.

In crossing the Huebra [17 Nov.], at San Muños, the enemy pressed our rear-guard very sharply, and we had some very heavy skirmishing. Sir E. Paget, by his own obstinacy in not believing the French Dragoons had intervened upon our line of march, was taken prisoner, and our rear-guard (my Brigade) driven from the ford. They had to take to the river as well as they were able, the soldiers leaping from a steep bank into it.

The sense and strength of my wife's Spanish horse were this day put to the test, for she had nothing for it but to make him leap into the river from the high bank, which the noble animal did, all fours like a dog. The poor Padre attempted the same, with the result that he and pony floated down the stream, and the pony was drowned, but his large Spanish capa or cloak kept him afloat, and he was dragged out by some of our soldiers. His holiness began now to think I had not exaggerated the hardships of a soldier's life. When well out of the river, he quietly asked my poor old West for a horse I always had ready to jump on in case my own were killed. West very quietly said.

"Never lend master's other fighting horse, not to nobody."

My wife interceded for the poor Padre, but had the same refusal.

Old West says, "We shan't march far; the river bothered us, it will stop the French. Our Riflemen don't mean to let those fellows over. Night and the walk will warm you."

I, seeing the distress my poor wife was likely to be in, had told her particularly to stay with the 52nd, thinking they would move into bivouac, while the Riflemen held the bed of the river where we had crossed, to which alone my attention was drawn. There was a ford, however, lower down the river, to which the 52nd were suddenly ordered. It was impassable, but in the enemy's attempt to cross, a heavy skirmish ensued, in which poor Captain Dawson was killed and forty or fifty men wounded; my wife in the thick of it, and the friar.

As soon as the ford was ascertained impassable, I was sent to bring back the 52nd, when, to my astonishment and alarm, I found my young wife drenched with leaping in the river, as much as from the torrents of rain above. The poor Padre might have been drawn for "the Knight of the Woeful Countenance." I brought the whole into our wet and miserable bivouac, and gave some Portuguese of my Brigade a dollar for a large fire, when, cold and shivery as she was, she laughed at the Padre. We had nothing to eat that night, as our mules were sent on, and there was this young and delicate creature, in the month of November in the north of Spain, wet as a drowned rat, with nothing to eat, and no cover from the falling deluge. Not a murmur escaped her but once. I had had no sleep for three nights, our rear being in a very ticklish position. In sitting by the fire I had fallen asleep, and fell between the fire and her. She had previously been roasted on one side, a cold mud on the other. This change of temperature awoke her, and for the only time in her life did she cry and say I might have avoided it. She had just woke out of her sleep, and when cold and shivery our feelings are acute. In a moment she exclaimed, "How foolish! you must have been nice and warm, and to know that is enough for me."

I took the Padre a mule; the rain broke, the little rivulet would soon be fordable, and at daylight the next morning we expected a regular squeeze from the enemy. To amend matters, too, in place of our moving off before daylight and getting a start, we were to follow the 1st Division, and this did not move. General Alten sent repeatedly to poor dear Sir William Stewart (who gave me my commission), to represent the prospect he had of a brush which ought to be avoided, when up rides to Charlie Beckwith, our A.Q.M.G., the Honourable Arthur Upton, saying:

"My dear Beckwith, you could not inform me where I could get a paysano (a peasant)? The 1st Division can't move; we have no guide."

"Oh, d—," says Charlie, "is that it? We will do anything to get you out of our way. Come to Harry Smith. He has a paysano, I know."

I always had three or four poor fellows in charge of a guard, so requisite are guides with light troops. I gave him his paysano, and by this time the sun was an hour high at least. To our delight, in place of a fight retreating, which partakes neither of the pomp nor majesty of war, but of nothing but hard and often inglorious losses, we saw the French army dismissed, all drying their clothes and as little in a state to attack as we were desirous of their company. We had a clear, cold, but unmolested long march, and fell in with some stores coming. Yesterday the soldier's life was one of misery, to-day all joy and elasticity!

Just as the rear-guard had moved off the ground, I heard the voice of a soldier familiar to me calling out:

"Oh, Mr. Smith!" (The Rifle soldiers ever called me "Mr. Smith.") "Don't leave me here." I rode up. As gallant a Rifleman as ever breathed, by name O'Donnell, lay there with his thigh fractured the day before by a cannon-shot. I was grieved for him. I had no means to assist him but one which I deemed it impossible he could avail himself of the tumbril of a gun. He said, "Oh, I can ride."

I galloped to Ross, who literally sent back with me a six-pounder, and took the poor fellow on the tumbril, the gunner cheerfully giving him his place. It was grievous to see poor O'Donnell hoisted up with his thigh smashed. We got him there, though, and he said:

"I shall do now." He died in two hours. I shall ever feel grateful to Ross; few men could have done it, but his guns were drawn by noble horses, and he was, and is, a *soldier*.

Over the bivouac fire this night the Padre became eloquent and sentimental.

"When you told me at Madrid what were the hardships and privations of a soldier's life in retreat, pursued by a vigorous enemy, I considered I had a very correct idea; I now see I had no conception whatever. But what appears to me so extraordinary is that every one acts for himself alone. There you see a poor knocked-up soldier sitting in the mud, unable to move; there come grooms with led horses. No one asks the sick man to ride, no one sympathizes with the other's feelings -- in short, every one appears to struggle against difficulties for himself alone."

I could see the Padre had not forgotten my old man West's refusal of my second war-horse.

On the day following [19 Nov.], the weather was clear but bitterly cold We reached the suburbs of Ciudad Rodrigo, happy enough to know that for this campaign the fighting was over. Although some of our troops had a long march before them into Portugal, we Light Division gentlemen were close at home. Many of our stoutest officers were sick, John Bell, Charlie Eeles, etc., and we had many wounded to look after. The Padre and my cheerful, light-hearted wife were cooking in a little house all day long. The Padre was a capital cook, and equally good when the food was prepared. I went out coursing every day, and some of our regiment fellows, notwithstanding the "retreat" and its hardships, went out duck-shooting, up to their middles in water, Jonathan Leach among the rest.

My brigade was ordered into our old villages of Alameda, Fuentes d'Oñoro, Guinaldo, and to march via San Felices el chico, there to cross the Agueda. The weather was very rainy and cold, but my vivacious little wife was full of animation and happiness, and the Padre usually cooking.

Fuentes d'Oñoro was to be the head-quarters of our Brigade. General Vandeleur took up his quarters in the Curé's house, around which in the battle had been a sanguinary conflict. I was at the other end of the village for the sake of an excellent stable. It belonged to the father of the beautiful Maria Josefa, who fled from her father's house with a commissary, was infamously treated by him, returned to her father's house, and was received by the good old man kindly, although with nearly a broken heart. Songs were sung about her all over Spain, and she was universally condemned, pitied, and pardoned. I put the Padre in this house, told him the tale of woe, and, to his credit, he did everything a Christian clergyman ought, to urge on the parents pardon of the ill-used penitent. Nor did he plead in vain, the poor thing was forgiven by every one but herself. The Padre requested my generous-hearted wife to see her, and this was a consolation to poor Maria Josefa worth a general action to behold.

My billet was some little distance from the stable, and while there my landlord married a second wife. The inhabitants of this part of Spain are very peculiar and primitive in their manners, dress, and customs; they are called Charras. The dress of the women is most costly, and a marriage feast exceeds any feast that I ever saw, or that has been described by Abyssinian Bruce. We had fun and much feasting for three days. One of the ceremonies is that during a dance in which the bride is, of course, the prima donna, her relatives and friends make her presents, which she receives while dancing in the most graceful, though rustic, attitudes. The presents are frequently considerable sums in gold, or gold and silver ornaments of singular workmanship. All relatives and friends give something, or it is regarded as a slight. My wife, who learned to dance the rustic measure on purpose, presented a doubloon in the most elegant and graceful manner, to the delight of her compatriots around, although, being an Estremenha, she was regarded by these primitive, but hospitable and generous, creatures, as half a foreigner. The bride has a knife in her uplifted hand, upon it an apple, and the smaller presents are presented by cutting the apple, and placing in the cut the money or ornament.

In this part of Spain the pigs are fed most delicately; they are driven first into woods of cork trees, which produce beautiful, sweet acorns, then into woods of magnificent chestnut trees, the keeper getting into the trees and flogging down the acorns and chestnuts with an immense long whip. The pigs thus fed yield a meat different from the usual meat of the animal. They are of a beautiful breed, become exceedingly fat, and the season of killing them and making black puddings and sausages for the year's supply is one of continual feasting. The peasants also cure the meat along each side of the backbone called loma de puerco. This they do in a very peculiar manner with salt, red pepper, and of course a soupçon of garlic in a thick slice; and, notwithstanding the little garlic, when simply boiled, it is the most delicious food, for breakfast particularly, that even a French cook could boast of.

During our stay at Fuentes, many were the rides my wife took on her horse Tiny to our friends in the different villages. At last, however, an order came to our Brigade head-quarters to vacate Fuentes d' Oñoro, as it was required for a part of the head-quarters establishment not far off at Freneda, and we moved to Guinaldo, to our deep regret. The Padre a few days before had taken his departure for his living at Vicalbaro. Two most magnificent mules, and his servant, came for him. We parted with mutual regret, but I am sorry to say he only wrote to us twice afterwards, and once to ask a favour for some individual.

At this time I was sporting mad. The Duke had a capital pack of fox-hounds. James Stewart, my chum, our A.Q.M.G., had an excellent pack of harriers to which I acted as whipper-in. After a very severe run, swimming two rivers, my Andalusian, which produced the doubloons at Alcala, died soon after he got back to his stable. Mr. Commissary Haines, at head-quarters, had a beautiful pack of little beagles. I was too proud to look at them. I had the best greyhounds in the world, -- "Moro," and some of his almost equally celebrated sons.

Chapter 11

Campaign of 1813 -- Battle of Vittoria

At Guinaldo we soon saw it was requisite to prepare for another campaign, and without any previous warning whatever, we received, about twelve at night, an order to march, which we did at daylight [21 May, 1813], and marched nineteen successive days without one halt.

I commenced this campaign under very unfortunate circumstances as far as my stud was concerned. I had five capital horses, and only two fit for work. Tiny, my wife's noble little horse, had received a violent injury from the pulling down of the bullock-manger (an immensely heavy timber, with mere holes in it for the ox's muzzle), when the extreme end and sharp point fell on his off fore-hoof, and he was so lame he could hardly travel to Vittoria. This was an awful loss to my wife. General Vandeleur now and then mounted me, or I should have been badly off indeed. James Stewart gave me a celebrated English hunter called "Old Chap." He had picked up a nail in his hind foot, and was not fit to ride for months, and an English mare had thrown out a ring-bone. (I must observe that winter quarters to my stud was no holiday.)

The march from Guinaldo to Palencia and thence to Vittoria was exceedingly interesting; the weather delightful; supplies, the mainspring of happiness in a soldier's life, plentiful; and never was any army (although the Duke had so censured us after the retreat from Burgos) inspired with such confidence in their leader, and such dependence on their own prowess. All was cheerfulness, joy, and anticipation. On reaching Toro [2 June], we found the bridge over the Douro destroyed. The river was full and barely fordable for cavalry and baggage animals. The bridge was partially repaired, some boats collected, and by boats our artillery, baggage, and material crossed, some of the infantry in boats, some scrambling over the bridge. The Douro, a magnificent and deep flowing river, was much up for the time of year. The passage was a most animating spectacle; it would have been a difficulty to an inexperienced army. With us, we were ordered to cross, and it was a matter of fun and excitement. No halt of Divisions, the river was crossed, and the day's march completed. My wife's dear Spaniard being lame, she rode a thoroughbred mare, which I gave £140 for, an elegant animal, but it no more had the sagacity of Tiny than a cur has that of a foxhound, and the day before we reached Palencia, upon a greasy bank, the mare slipped up and fell upon my poor wife and broke a small bone in her foot. This was to me an awful accident; heretofore health and happiness facilitated all; now, but for her natural vivacity and devotion, such was the pain, she must have remained at Palencia, and we must have separated.

The bare idea aroused all her energy, and she said, "Get me a mule or an ass, and put a Spanish saddle for a lady on it; my feet will rest upon the foot-board, and go I will!"

Dozens of officers were in immediate requisition, some trying mules to find a very easy one, others running from shop to shop to get a good easy and well-cushioned saddle. There was no difficulty. The word "stay behind" was the talisman to move pain, and the mule was put in progress next morning with that success determination ever ensures, for "Where there's a will, there's a way."

The whole of the Duke's army passed this day through the narrow main street of rather a pretty city, Palencia [7 June]. From a little after daylight, until past six in the evening, there was a continued stream of men -- cavalry, artillery, infantry, and baggage, without a moment's interruption the whole day. To view this torrent of life was a sight which made an indelible impression upon a beholder.

But to my wounded wife. At the end of the march, the Brigade head-quarters went, as usual, into the village near the bivouac. Oh, the ceremony of her dismounting, the quantity of officers' cloaks spread for her reception; the "Take care! Now I'll carry the leg," of the kind-hearted doctor! Talk of Indian attention! Here were a set of fellows ready to lay down their lives even to alleviate momentary pain.

As we approached Burgos, the scene of previous failure, we Light, 3rd, and 4th Divisions expected the reluctant honour of besieging it, and so flushed with hope were we to meet the enemy in an open field and not behind bastions, curtains, embrasures, and defences, we fairly wished Burgos at the devil.

The day we were moving upon it [13 June] (the Duke knew it would not be defended), to our delight, one, two, three, four terrific explosions took place, and well did we know the enemy had blown Burgos to where we wished it. The universal joy was most manifest, for, if we had besieged it, former failure would have excited these crack Divisions to get into it with the determination they had ever previously evinced, but the blowing it up happily got us out of the difficulty to our hearts' content.

My wife's foot gradually improved, and in a few days she was on her horse again, and en route in the column; for the soldiers, although generally averse to be interfered with by horses on the line of march, were ever delighted to get her to ride with their Company. Seeing her again on her horse was a great relief to my mind, for, in her peculiar and isolated position, the bare surmise of our separation was horrid, and, if I must have left her behind, the fact of a true Catholic allying herself to a heretic would, among bigoted inhabitants, have secured her anything but tender attention.

Our Division at San Millan, near Vittoria [18 June], intercepted the route of one of the French Columns as it was retiring into their position at Vittoria, and had as brilliant a fight entirely of our own as any one throughout the campaign. Some of the 1st Hussars also had a severe brush. Our Division halted the next day [20th], but the army never did, from the day of breaking up its cantonments until they fought the battle of Vittoria. It was a most wonderful march, the army in great fighting order, and every man in better wind than a trained pugilist.

At the Battle of Vittoria [21 June] my Brigade, in the middle of the action, was sent to support the 7th Division, which was very hotly engaged. I was sent forward to report myself to Lord Dalhousie, who commanded. I found his lordship and his Q.M.G., Drake, an old Rifle comrade, in deep conversation. I reported pretty quick, and asked for orders (the head of my Brigade was just getting under fire).

I repeated the question, "What orders, my Lord?"

Drake became somewhat animated, and I heard His Lordship say:

"Better to take the village," which the French held with twelve guns (I had counted by their fire), and seemed to be inclined to keep it.

I roared out, "Certainly, my Lord," and off I galloped, both calling to me to come back, but, as none are so deaf as those who won't hear, I told General Vandeleur we were immediately to take the village.

There was no time to lose, and the 52nd Regiment deployed into line as if at Shorncliffe, while our Riflemen were sent out in every direction, five or six deep, keeping up a fire nothing could resist. I galloped to the officer commanding a Battalion in the 7th Division (the 82nd, I think).

"Lord Dalhousie desires you closely to follow this Brigade of the Light Division."

"Who are you, sir?"

"Never mind that; disobey my Lord's order at your peril."

My Brigade, the 52nd in line and the swarms of Riflemen, rushed at the village, and although the ground was intersected in its front by gardens and ditches, nothing ever checked us until we reached the rear of the village, where we halted to reform -- the twelve guns, tumbrils, horses, etc., standing in our possession. There never was a more impetuous onset -- nothing could withstand such a burst of determination. Before we were ready to pursue the enemy -- for we Light Division ever reformed and got into order before a second attack, thanks to poor General Bob Craufurd's most excellent tuition -- up came Lord Dalhousie with his Q.M.G., Drake, to old Vandeleur, exclaiming:

"Most brilliantly achieved indeed! Where is the officer you sent to me for orders?"

"Here I am, my lord." Old Drake knew well enough.

"Upon my word, sir, you receive and carry orders quicker than any officer I ever saw."

"You said, 'Take the village.' My lord, there it is," I said, "guns and all."

He smiled, and old Drake burst into one of his grins, "Well done, Harry."

We were hotly engaged all the afternoon pursuing the French over very broad ditches. Until we neared Vittoria to our left, there was a plain free from ditches. The confusion of baggage, etc., was indescribable. Our Brigade was moving rapidly on, when such a swarm of French Cavalry rushed out from among the baggage into our skirmishers, opposite a company of the 2nd Battalion Rifle Brigade, commanded by Lieutenant Tom Cochrane, we thought they must have been swept off. Fortunately for Tom, a little rough ground and a bank enabled him to command his Company to lie down, and such a reception they gave the horsemen, while some of our Company were flying to their support, that the French fled with a severe loss. Our Riflemen were beautiful shots, and as undaunted as bulldogs. We knew so well, too, how to support each other, that scarcely had the French Dragoons shown themselves when Cochrane's rear was supported, and we had such mutual confidence in this support that we never calculated on disaster, but assumed the boldest front and bearing.

A rather curious circumstance occurred to me after the first heights and the key of the enemy's central position was carried. I was standing with Ross's Brigade of guns sharply engaged, when my horse fell as if stone dead. I jumped off, and began to look for the wound. I could see none, and gave the poor animal a kick on the nose. He immediately shook his head, and as instantly jumped on his legs, and I on his back. The artillerymen all said it was the current of air, or, as they call it, the wind, of one of the enemy's cannon-shot. On the attack on the village previously described, Lieutenant Northey (52nd Regiment) was not knocked off as I was, but he was knocked down by the wind of a shot, and his face as black as if he had been two hours in a pugilistic ring.

The fall of my horse had been observed by some of our soldiers as they were skirmishing forward, and a report soon prevailed that I was killed, which, in the course of the afternoon, was communicated to my poor wife, who followed close to the rear on the very field of battle, crossing the plain covered with treasure. Her old groom, West, proposed to carry off some on a led horse. She said:

"Oh, West, never mind money. Let us look for your master." She had followed the 1st Brigade men, the 2nd having been detached, unobserved by her, to aid the 7th Division.

After the battle, at dusk, my Brigade was ordered to join the 1st Brigade, with General Alten's head-quarters. I had lost my voice from the exertion of cheering with our men (not cheering them on, for they required no such example), and as I approached the 1st Brigade, to take up the ground for mine, I heard my wife's lamentations. I immediately galloped up to her, and spoke to her as well as I could, considering the loss of my voice.

"Oh, then, thank God, you are not killed, only badly wounded."

"Thank God," I growled, "I am neither," but, in her ecstasy of joy, this was not believed for a long while.

After putting up my Brigade (we required no picquets, the Cavalry were far in our front in pursuit of the flying enemy) we, that is, my General and Staff, repaired to a barn, where we got in our horses and some forage, and lay down among them. It was dark; we had no lights, and sleep after such a day was as refreshing as eating, even if we had any means.

At daybreak our luggage had arrived, and we were busy preparing some breakfast. Hardly did the kettle boil when "Fall in!" was the word. Just as we were jumping on our horses, my young wife, her ears being rather quick, said:

"I am sure I hear some one moaning, like a wounded man."

We looked round, and I saw there was a loft for hay over our barn. I immediately scrambled up with assistance, for the ladder, like Robinson Crusoe's, had been hauled up. When I reached the landing-place, such a scene met my eye! Upwards of twenty French officers, all more or less severely wounded, one poor fellow in the agony of death, and a lady, whom I recognized as Spanish, grieving over him.

At first the poor fellows funked. I soon assured them of every safety and protection, and put my wife and the poor Spanish lady, her countrywoman, in communication. All we could spare, or, rather, all our breakfast, was given to the wounded, for march we must. The General sent his A.D.C. for a guard; we did all we could at the moment, and the poor fellows were grateful indeed. The Spanish lady had a most beautiful little pug dog, a thoroughbred one, with a very extraordinary collar of bells about its neck. She insisted upon my wife's accepting the dog as a token of gratitude for our kindness. The little animal was accepted immediately, and named "Vittoria"; we jumped on our horses, and parted for ever, gratified, however, at having had it in our power to render this slight assistance to the poor fellows wounded and in distress. The dog became afterwards a celebrated animal in the Division, universally known and caressed, and the heroine of many a little anecdote. It was the most sensible little brute Nature ever produced, and it and Tiny became most attached friends.

On this day's march our soldiers could scarcely move -- men, in such wind and health as they were -- but the fact is they had got some flocks of the enemy's sheep, and fallen in with a lot of flour; they had eaten till they were gorged like vultures, and every man's haversack was laden with flour and raw meat, all of which, except a day or two's supply, the Generals of Brigade were obliged to order to be thrown away. We were soon, however, close on the heels of the enemy, and the first shot revived the power to march. The retreat of the enemy was marked by every excess and atrocity and villages burning in every direction.

We Light Division had the pleasure, ere we reached Pamplona, to take the enemy's only remaining gun.

Chapter 12

Campaign of 1813 -- Advance to Toverra

The night before we reached Pamplona [24 June], the enemy, rather unexpectedly to us, drove in the picquets of my Brigade in a very sharp skirmish, although we were as ever prepared, and the Division got under arms. This convinced us that the whole army, except the garrison at Pamplona, was in full retreat into France. It is a peculiar custom of the French unexpectedly to put back your picquets when they are about to retire; that is, when the ground admits no obstacle of bridge, river, or village, intervening. The object of such forward moves I have never heard satisfactorily given.

On this evening a stout French gentleman came in to our advanced post, saying he wanted to see the Duke. I took him to General Vandeleur. He dined with us, and a most jawing, facetious fellow he was. At first we regarded him as a spy, which he afterwards told General Vandeleur he was, and in the employ of the Duke. He could not proceed that night, for we did not know in the least where head-quarters were, and the night was excessively dark; so the French gentleman, whom I wished at the devil, was given in charge to me. If he had had any inclination to escape I defied him, for I put some of our old vigilant Riflemen around him, so that not a man could get in or out of the room I had put him in. We afterwards heard my friend was a man of great use to the Duke, and one of King Joseph's household.

The next day [25 June] we Light Division passed Pamplona, leaving it by a very intricate road to our right, and were cantoned in the village of Offala. It was necessary to keep a look-out towards Pamplona, and my General, Vandeleur, and I rode to look where to post our picquets. I had a most athletic and active fellow with me as a guide, very talkative, and full of the battle of Vittoria. He asked me what was the name of the General before us.

I said, "General Vandeleur."

I heard him muttering it over to himself several times. He then ran up to the General, and entered into conversation. The General soon called me to him, for he could not speak a word of Spanish.

"What's the fellow say?"

"He is telling all he heard from the Frenchmen who were billeted in his house in the retreat. He is full of anecdote."

He then looked most expressively in Vandeleur's face, and says, "Yes, they say the English fought well, but had it not been for one General Bandelo, the French would have gained the day."

"How the devil did this fellow know?" says Vandeleur.

I never undeceived the General, and he fancies to this day his Brigade's being sent to assist the 7th Division was the cause of the Frenchmen's remark. My guide, just like a "cute" Irishman or American, gave me a knowing wink.

This very fellow turned out to be owner of the house my wife and baggage and I got into -- the General's Aide-de-camp, as was often the case, having shown her into one near the General. After I had dressed myself, he came to me and said:

"When you dine, I have some capital wine, as much as you and your servants like; but," he says, "come down and look at my cellar."

The fellow had been so civil, I did not like to refuse him. We descended by a stone staircase, he carrying a light. He had upon his countenance a most sinister expression. I saw something exceedingly excited him: his look became fiend-like. He and I were alone, but such confidence had we Englishmen in a Spaniard, and with the best reason, that I apprehended no personal evil. Still his appearance was very singular.

When we got to the cellar-door, he opened it, and held the light so as to show the cellar; when, in a voice of thunder, and with an expression of demoniacal hatred and antipathy, pointing to the floor, he exclaimed:

"There lie four of the devils who thought to subjugate Spain! I am a Navarrese. I was born free from all foreign invasion, and this right hand shall plunge this stiletto in my own heart as it did into theirs, ere I and my countrymen are subjugated!"

I see the excited patriot as I write. Horror-struck as I was, the instinct of self-preservation induced me to admire the deed exceedingly, while my very frame quivered and my blood was frozen, to see the noble science of war and the honour and chivalry of arms reduced to the practices of midnight assassins. Upon the expression of my admiration, he cooled, and while he was deliberately drawing wine for my dinner, which, however strange it may be, I drank with the gusto its flavour merited, I examined the four bodies. They were Dragoons -- four athletic, healthy-looking fellows.

As we ascended, he had perfectly recovered the equilibrium of his vivacity and naturally good humour. I asked him how he, single-handed, had perpetrated this deed on four armed men (for their swords were by their sides).

"Oh, easily enough. I pretended to love a Frenchman" (or, in his words, 'I was an Afrancesado'), "and I proposed, after giving them a good dinner, we should drink to the extermination of the English." He then looked at me and ground his teeth. "The French rascals, they little guessed what I contemplated. Well, we got into the cellar, and drank away until I made them so drunk, they fell, and my purpose was easily, and as joyfully, effected." He again brandished his dagger, and said, "Thus die all enemies to Spain."

Their horses were in his stable. When the French Regiment marched off he gave these to some guerrillas in the neighbourhood. It is not difficult to reconcile with truth the assertion of the historian who puts down the loss of the French army, during the Spanish war, as 400,000 men, for more men fell in this midnight manner than by the broad-day sword, or the pestilence of climate, which in Spain, in the autumn, is excessive.

The next day we marched a short distance to a beautiful village, or town, rather, -- Villalba, where we halted a day, and expected to remain three or four. It was on a Sunday afternoon, and some of the recollection of the Sunday of our youth was passing across the mind of the lover of his family and his country -- the very pew at church, the old peasants in the aisle; the friendly neighbours' happy faces; the father, mother, brothers, sisters; the joys, in short, of home, for, amidst the eventful scenes of such a life, recollection will bring the past in view, and compare the blessings of peace with the horror, oh! the cruel horror, of war! In the midst of this mental soliloquy, my dear wife exclaims:

"Mi Enrique, how thoughtful you look!"

I dare not tell her that my thoughts reverted to my home. Hers being a desolate waste, the subject was ever prohibited, for her vivacious mind, and her years of juvenile excitement, could never control an excess of grief if the words, "your home," ever escaped my lips.

My reverie was soon aroused by the entrance of a soldier, without ceremony -- for every one was ever welcome.

"Sir, is the order come?"

"For what?" I said. "An extra allowance of wine?"

"No," he said, "for an extra allowance of marching. We are to be off directly after these French chaps, as expects to get to France without a kick from the Light Division."

I was aware he alluded to General Clausel's division that was retiring by the pass over the Pyrenees, called La Haca. It is most singular, but equally true, that our soldiers knew every move in contemplation long before any officer. While we were in conversation, in came the order; away went all thoughts of home, and a momentary regret on quitting so nice a quarter was banished in the excitement of the march.

In twenty minutes our Division was in full march to try and intercept Clausel's Division. That night we marched most rapidly to Tafalla, next day to Olite, thence brought up our right shoulder towards Sanguessa. This was a night-march of no ordinary character to all, particularly to me and my wife. Her Spanish horse, Tiny, was so far recovered from his lameness that she insisted on riding him. On a night-march we knew the road to be difficult. In crossing the Arragon [30 June], although the bridge was excellent, on this march by some singular accident (it was very dark and raining) an interval occurred in our column -- a thing unprecedented, so particular were we, thanks to Craufurd's instructions -- and the majority of the Division, in place of crossing the bridge, passed the turn and went on a league out of the direction. My Brigade was leading. Two Battalions came all right, and I stayed more at the head of the column than was my wont, to watch the guides. So dark and intricate was the road we were moving on, I proposed to the General to form up, and see that our troops were all right. After the two first Battalions formed, I waited a short time in expectation of the next, the 2nd Battalion of the Rifle Brigade. I hallooed, seeing no column, when a voice a long way off answered. It was that of the most extraordinary character, the eccentric Colonel Wade.

I galloped up, and said, "Colonel, form up your Battalion, so soon as you reach the Brigade."

"By Jesus," he said, "we are soon formed; I and my bugler are alone."

I, naturally somewhat excited, asked, "Where's the Regiment?"

"Upon my soul, and that's what I would like to ask you."

I then saw some mistake must have happened.

I galloped back in the dark to the bridge, saw no column whatever, but heard voices far beyond the bridge. The column, after passing it in the dark, had discovered the error and were coming back.

Meanwhile, my wife heard me hallooing and came towards me. I had dismounted, and was leading my horse a little way off the road up the left bank of the Arragon; the rain was falling in torrents, the bank of the river gave way under me, and a flash of lightning at the moment showed me I was falling into the bed of the river about thirty feet below. I had firmly hold of my bridle -- the avalanche frightened my noble horse (the celebrated "Old Chap," the hunter that James Stewart gave me); he flew round and dragged me from inevitable perdition.

My wife and old West were close behind at the moment, and she witnessed the whole, equally to her horror and satisfaction. Then such a tale of woe from herself.

The uneven ground at night had so lamed her dear little horse, Tiny, that he could not carry her. She got off in the rain and dark, herself still excessively lame from the broken bone in the foot, and literally crawled along, until the rocky road improved, and West again put her upon her faithful Tiny. I could devote neither time nor attention to her. Day was just beginning to break. I directed her to the bivouac, and most energetically sought to collect my Brigade, which, with the daylight, I soon effected. When I got back, I found my wife sitting, holding her umbrella over General Vandeleur (who was suffering dreadfully from rheumatism in the shoulder in which he had been wounded at the storm of Ciudad Rodrigo), recounting to him her night's adventures and laughing heartily. The weather totally precluded any possibility of our molesting Clausel, and we were ordered to march to Sanguessa, which we did the following day, and Charlie Gore, General Kempt's A.D.C., gave a ball [1 July], where there was as much happiness as if we were at Almack's, and some as handsome women, the loves of girls of Sanguessa.

That night's march was the most extraordinary thing which ever occurred to our organized Light Division. We all blamed each other, but the fact is the turn of the road to the bridge was abrupt, the night dark, the road so narrow that staff-officers could not ride up and down the flank of the column; it may be regarded as "an untoward event."

From Sanguessa we made rather long marches for the Valle of San Estevan, through a most beautiful country covered in a great measure with immense chestnut trees. After we had halted a day or two [7-14 July] in this valley, of which the beauty is not to be conceived, we marched on towards Vera by a road along the banks of the river Bidassoa. At Vera, the enemy had fortified a large house very strongly, and their picquets were upon its line. On our advance, we put back the enemy's picquets, but not without a sharp skirmish, and we held the house that afternoon.

In front of the mountain of Santa Barbara was a very steep hill, which the enemy held in force, but a dense fog of the mountains prevented us seeing each other. Colonel Barnard, with the 1st Battalion Rifle Brigade, was sent to dislodge them [15 July]. They proved to be three or four times his numbers. His attack, however, was supported, and as he himself describes it, "I hallooed the fellows off in the fog."

We had a good many men and officers, however, severely wounded. The next day, or in the night, the enemy abandoned the fortified house of the large village of Vera in their front, retired behind the village, and firmly established themselves on the heights, while we occupied Vera with some sick officers, our picquets being posted beyond. The enemy's vedettes and ours for many days were within talking distance, yet we never had an alert by night or by day.

Chapter 13

Campaign of 1813 -- In the Pyrenees -- General Skerrett -- Combat of Vera -- Fight at the Bridge, and Death of Cadoux

Just before we reached Vera, my dear friend and General, Vandeleur, was moved to a Cavalry Brigade, and General Skerrett, a very different man, was sent to us, with a capital fellow for an A.D.C. -- Captain Fane, or, as usually designated, "Ugly Tom." I, who had been accustomed to go in and out of my previous Generals' tents and quarters as my own, and either breakfast or dine as I liked, was perfectly thunderstruck when it was intimated to me I was to go only when asked; so Tom the A.D.C. and we lived together, to the great amusement of my wife, who was always playing Tom some trick or other.

During our halt in this position, the siege of San Sebastian was going on. Soult, an able officer, who had been appointed to the command of the beaten French force, soon reorganized it, and instilled its old pride of victory, and inspired all again with the ardour and vivacity of French soldiers. The siege of San Sebastian was vigorously prosecuted. Pamplona was closely invested, and, from want of provisions, must inevitably ere long surrender. Soult, therefore, had a brilliant opportunity either to raise the siege of San Sebastian, or to throw supplies in to Pamplona, or to do both, if great success attended his operations. This opportunity he ably availed himself of, by making a rapid movement to our right to the Pass of Roncesvalles of knightly fame, and obliging the Duke of Wellington to concentrate a great part of his army to protect Pamplona, or, rather, to ensure its strict blockade, while the siege of San Sebastian was for the time suspended, awaiting supplies which were on their passage from England. My Division, the Light, was kept between the two, as were Lord Dacre's cavalry, and we had some very harassing marches, when it was discovered Soult had penetrated the

Pyrenees and was resolved on a general action. This he fought on the 27th and 28th July, with the Frenchman's usual success, a good thrashing.

The Light Division made a terrible night march on this occasion, one of the most fatiguing to the soldiers that I ever witnessed. On the Pyrenees, as on other mountains, the darkness is indescribable. We were on a narrow mountain path, frequently with room only for one or two men, when a soldier of the Rifle Brigade rolled down a hill as nearly perpendicular as may be. We heard him bumping along, pack, rifle, weight of ammunition, etc., when from the bottom he sang out, "Halloa there! Tell the Captain there's not a bit of me alive at all; but the devil a bone have I broken; and faith I'm thinking no soldier ever came to his ground at such a rate before. Have a care, boys, you don't follow. The breach at Badajos was nothing to the bottomless pit I'm now in."

After the battles of the Pyrenees, our Division was pushed forward with great rapidity to intercept the retreat of one of the corps d' armée, and General Kempt's -- the 1st -- Brigade had some very heavy fighting [at Jansi, 1 Aug.]; while at [Echallar], poor General Barnes, now no more, in command of a Brigade of the 7th Division, made one of the boldest and most successful attacks on five times his number, but one in which bravery and success far exceeded judgment or utility.

We moved on again, and on one of our marches came to some very nice cottages, one of which fell to the lot of myself and Tom Fane, the A.D.C. The poor peasant was a kind-hearted farmer of the mountains, his fields highly cultivated, his farmyard supplied with poultry; every domestic comfort his situation in life demanded was his -- poor fellow, he merited all. He killed some ducks for our supper, his garden supplied beautiful peas, and we had a supper royalty would have envied with our appetites. My wife had spread her cloak on the floor -- she was perfectly exhausted -- and was fast asleep. I awoke her, she ate a capital supper, but the next morning upbraided me and Tom Fane for not having given her anything to eat; and to this day she is unconscious of sitting at our supper-table. Judge by this anecdote what real fatigue is. The next morning we could hardly induce our host to receive payment for his eggs, his poultry, his bread, bacon, peas, milk, etc., and he would insist on giving my wife a beautiful goat in full milk, which was added to the boy Antonio's herd. We marched with mutual feelings of newly-acquired but real friendship.

Three days afterwards, we returned to the very same ground, and we again occupied our previous dear little mountain retreat, but the accursed hand of war had stamped devastation upon it. The beautiful fields of Indian corn were all reaped as forage, the poultry yard was void, the produce of our peasant's garden exhausted, his flour all consumed -- in a word, he had nothing left of all his previous plenty but a few milch goats, and that night he, poor thing, supped with us from the resources of our rations and biscuit. He said the French had swept off everything the English did not require. The latter paid for everything, and gave him bons or receipts for the Indian corn reaped as forage, which he knew some day our commissary would take up and pay. I never pitied man more, and in the midst of his affliction it was beautiful to observe a pious resignation and a love for his country, when he exclaimed, "Gracias a Dios, you have driven back the villainous French to their own country."

We returned to our line on this side of Vera, and the siege of San Sebastian was again vigorously resumed. We Light Division, with the 3rd and 4th, were out of that glory, which we did not regret, although the Duke never took the town until he sent to these three Divisions for volunteers for the storming party [31 Aug.]. Then we soon took it; but in candour I should state that the breaches were rendered more practicable than when first stormed, the defences destroyed, and the enemy's means of defence diminished. It was, however, still a tough piece of work, in which we lost some valuable officers and soldiers. The enemy made a forward movement [the same day, 31 Aug.] for the purpose of reinforcing the garrison, and in the morning put back our picquets, and we anticipated a general action. However, the whole of the enemy moved to the Lower Bidassoa, and crossed in force. The day was very rainy, and the river was so full the French were compelled to retreat rapidly; in fact, so sudden was the rise of the river, many were obliged to retire by the bridge in our possession.

My new General -- who, I soon discovered, was by nature a gallant Grenadier, and no Light Troop officer, which requires the eye of a hawk and the power of anticipating the enemy's intention -- who was always to be found off his horse, standing in the most exposed spot under the enemy's fire while our Riflemen were well concealed, as stupidly composed for himself as inactive for the welfare of his command. When the enemy put back our picquets in the morning, it was evidently their intention to possess themselves of the bridge, which was curiously placed as regarded our line of picquets. Thus --

We did not occupy Vera, but withdrew on our own side of it, and I saw the enemy preparing to carry the houses near the bridge in the occupation of the 2nd Battalion Rifle Brigade. I said:

"General Skerrett, unless we send down the 52nd Regiment in support, the enemy will drive back the Riflemen. They cannot hold those houses against the numbers prepared to attack. Our men will fight like devils expecting to be supported, and their loss, when driven out, will be very severe."

He laughed (we were standing under a heavy fire exposed) and said, "Oh, is that your opinion?"

I said -- most impertinently, I admit, -- "And it will be yours in five minutes," for I was by no means prepared to see the faith in support, which so many fights had established, destroyed, and our gallant fellows knocked over by a stupidity heretofore not exemplified.

We had scarcely time to discuss the matter when down came a thundering French column with swarms of sharpshooters, and, as I predicted, drove our people out of the houses with one fell swoop, while my General would move nothing on their flank or rear to aid them. We lost men and some officers, and the enemy possessed the houses, and consequently, for the moment, possessed the passage of the bridge. From its situation, however, it was impossible they could maintain it, unless they put us farther back by a renewed attack on our elevated position. So I said:

"You see now what you have permitted, general and we must retake these houses, which we ought never to have lost."

He quietly said, "I believe you are right."

I could stand this no longer, and I galloped up to Colonel Colborne, in command of that beautiful 52nd Regiment, who was as angry as he soon saw I was.

"Oh, sir, it is melancholy to see this. General Skerrett will do nothing; we must retake those houses. I told him what would happen."

"I am glad of it, for I was angry with you."

In two seconds we retook the houses, for the enemy, seeing our determination to hold them, was aware the nature of the ground would not enable him to do so unless he occupied the position we intended to defend, and his effort was as much as not to see whether we were in earnest, or whether, when attacked in force, we should retire. The houses were retaken, as I said, and the firing ceased the whole afternoon.

The evening came on very wet. We knew that the enemy had crossed the Bidassoa [31 Aug.], and that his retreat would be impossible from the swollen state of the river. We knew pretty well the Duke would shove him into the river if he could; this very bridge, therefore, was of the utmost importance, and no exertion should have been spared on our part so to occupy it after dark as to prevent the passage being seized. The rain was falling in torrents. I proposed that the whole of the 2nd Battalion Rifle Brigade should be posted in the houses, the bridge should be barricaded, and the 52nd Regiment should be close at hand in support. Skerrett positively laughed outright, ordered the whole Battalion into our position, but said:

"You may leave a picquet of one officer and thirty men at the bridge." He was in the house on the heights he had previously occupied. I had a little memorandum-book in my pocket; I took it out for the first time in my life to note my General's orders. I read what he said, asking if that was his order. He said, "Yes, I have already told you so."

I said most wickedly, "We shall repent this before daylight." He was callous to anything. I galloped down to the houses, ordered the Battalion to retire, and told my brother Tom, the Adjutant, to call to me a picquet of an officer and thirty men for the bridge. Every officer and soldier thought I was mad.

Tom said, "Cadoux's company is for picquet."

Up rode poor Cadoux, a noble soldier, who could scarcely believe what I said, but began to abuse me not supporting them in the morning.

I said, "Scold away, all true; but no fault of mine. But come, no time for jaw, the picquet!"

Cadoux, noble fellow, says, "My company is so reduced this morning, I will stay with it if I may. There are about fifty men."

I gladly consented, for I had great faith in Cadoux's ability and watchfulness, and I told him he might rest assured he would be attacked an hour or two before daylight.

He said, "Most certainly I shall, and I will now strengthen myself, and block up the bridge as well as I can, and I will, if possible, hold the bridge until supported; so, when the attack commences, instantly send the whole Battalion to me, and, please God, I will keep the bridge."

It was then dark, and I rode as fast as I could to tell Colborne, in whom we had all complete faith and confidence. He was astonished, and read my memorandum. We agreed that, so soon as the attack commenced, his Battalion should move down the heights on the flank of the 2nd Battalion Rifle Brigade, which would rush to support Cadoux, and thus we parted, I as sulky as my hot nature would admit, knowing some disaster would befall my dear old Brigade heretofore so judiciously handled.

In the course of the night, as we were lying before the fire, I far from asleep, General Skerrett received a communication from General Alten to the purport "that the enemy were retiring over the swollen river; it was, therefore, to be apprehended he would before daylight endeavour to possess himself of the bridge; that every precaution must be taken to prevent him." I, now being reinforced in opinion, said:

"Now, General, let me do so." As he was still as obstinate as ever, we were discussing the matter (I fear as far as I am concerned, very hotly) when the "En avant, en avant! L'Empereur récompensera le premier qu'avancera," was screeched into our very ears, and Cadoux's fire was hot as ever fifty men's was on earth.

"Now," says I, "General, who is right?" I knew what the troops would do. My only hope was that Cadoux could keep the bridge as he anticipated. The fire of the enemy was very severe, and the rushes of his columns most determined; still Cadoux's fire was from his post. Three successive times, with half his gallant band, did he charge and drive back the enemy over the bridge, the other half remaining in the houses as support. His hope and confidence in support and the importance of his position sustained him until a melancholy shot pierced his head, and he fell lifeless from his horse. A more gallant soul never left its mortal abode. His company at this critical moment were driven back; the French column and rearguard crossed, and, by keeping near the bed of the river, succeeded in escaping, although the Riflemen were in support of poor Cadoux with as much rapidity as distance allowed, and daylight saw Colborne where he said he would be.

I was soon at the bridge. Such a scene of mortal strife from the fire of fifty men was never witnessed. The bridge was almost choked with the dead; the enemy's loss was enormous, and many of his men were drowned, and all his guns were left in the river a mile or two below the bridge. The number of dead was so great, the bodies were thrown into the rapid stream in the hope that the current would carry them, but many rocks impeded them, and when the river subsided, we had great cause to lament our precipitancy in hurling the bodies, for the stench soon after was awful.

The Duke was awfully annoyed, as well he might be, but, as was his rule, never said anything when disaster could not be amended. I have never told my tale till now. Skerrett was a bilious fellow (a gallant Grenadier, I must readily avow), and I hope his annoyance so affected his liver it precipitated a step he had desired -- as his father was just dead, and he was heir to an immense property -- to retire home on sick-leave. You may rely on it, I threw no impediment in his way, for when he was gone, Colonel Colborne was my Brigadier, whom we all regarded inferior to no one but the Duke.

Many is the conversation he and I have had over the lamentable affair which killed poor Cadoux. I really believe, had he survived, he would have held the bridge, although the enemy attacked it in desperation, and although each time the column was driven back, a few men in the dark succeeded in crossing, and these fellows, all practised soldiers, posted themselves under cover on the banks of the river below the bridge, and caused the loss our people sustained, that of noble Cadoux among the rest, with impunity. Cadoux's manner was effeminate, and, as a boy, I used to quiz him. He and I were, therefore, although not enemies, not friends, until the battle of Vittoria, when I saw him most conspicuous. He was ahead of me on his gallant war horse, which he took at Barossa with holsters full of doubloons, as the story went. I was badly mounted that day, and my horse would not cross a brook which his was scrambling over. I leaped from my saddle over my horse's head (I was very active in those days), seized his horse by the tail, and I believe few, if any, were as soon in the middle of the Frenchmen's twelve guns as we were in support of the 7th Division. From that day we were comrades in every sense of the term, and I wept over his gallant remains with a bursting heart, as, with his Company who adored him, I consigned to the grave the last external appearance of Daniel Cadoux. His fame can never die.

The enemy retired into their previous position, as did we, and San Sebastian was ours. We were in this line for some time, daily watching the enemy making works with extraordinary vigour and diligence, which we knew ere long we should have the glory (the pleasure, to most of us) to run our heads against, for such was the ardour and confidence of our army at this moment, that, if Lord Wellington had told us to attempt to carry the moon, we should have done it.

During the occupation of our present position, I found the Basque inhabitants on the Spanish side, and those on the French side of the Pyrenees, carried on a sort of contraband trade, and that brandy and claret were to be had. One day, therefore, upon General Skerrett's complaining to me he could get no wine or sheep, I told him I could get him both. My smugglers were immediately in requisition. They got me eight sheep and one dozen of claret. I was disappointed at the small supply -- accustomed to hospitable old Vandeleur's consumption -- and I told my new General. He said he was exceedingly obliged to me; he should be glad of one sheep and two bottles of wine. It did not make a bad story through the Brigade. I and the A.D.C., Tom Fane, however, managed to consume all.

One day (the man may now be conceived) Skerrett gave a great dinner, and the liberal Barnard and Colborne, commanding Regiments in the Division, were asked to dine. Tom Fane and I were amused, for we knew he had but little to give them to eat and less to drink, and where were the materials to come from? And Barnard loved a good dinner, with at least two bottles of good wine. To my astonishment, when I waited on him, as I usually did every morning, for orders, he was dressed.

I said, "Where are you going, General?" (To me he was ever a most affable, and rather an amusing, fellow.)

He said, "To head-quarters at Lesaca."

So Tom and I supposed he would come back laden with supplies. (At head-quarters there was an excellent sutler, but the prices were, of course, beyond any moderate means.) So Tom, A.D.C., was on the look-out for his return. He soon arrived with a bottle of sherry in each pocket of his military blue coat, viz. two, and says:

"Fane, tell Smith, as my wine stock is not large, to be cautious of it."

Tom did tell me, and, when we met in the dining-room, the joke was too good not to tell such noble and liberal fellows as Barnard and Colborne. Down we sat to, oh! such a dinner; our soldiers in camp lived far better. So Barnard says:

"Being so near the French, we shall have plenty of cooks in camp soon; come, Smith, a glass of wine," and I think we drank the pocket two bottles in about as many minutes; when Barnard as funny a fellow and as noble a soldier as ever lived, says, "Now General, some more of this wine. We camp fellows do not get such a treat every day."

Barnard had a French cook, taken at the battle of Salamanca, and lived like a gentleman.

"Barnard," Skerrett says, looking like a fiend at me, "that is the last, I very much regret to say, of an old stock" (Barnard winked at me); "what I must now give you, I fear, won't be so good." It was produced; it was trash of some sort, but not wine.

"No," says Barnard, "that won't do, but let us have some brandy." We got some execrable coffee, and here ended the only feast he ever gave while in command of my Brigade.

Poor Skerrett, he soon inherited £7000 a year, not long to enjoy it. He was killed in the most brilliant, and at the same time the most unfortunate, affair that ever decorated and tarnished British laurels, at Bergen Op Zoom.

Chapter 14

Campaign of 1813 -- Colonel Colborne -- Second Combat of Vera

In our Division, generally speaking, the officers of each Company had a little mess of their own, an arrangement indispensable, so much detached were we on picquets, etc. Some of us lived most comfortably, and great interchange of hospitality existed. We all had goats, and every mess had a boy, who was in charge of them on the march and in quarters, and milked them. On the march the flock of each regiment and Brigade assembled and moved with their goat-herds, when each drove his master's goats to his quarters. We observed extraordinary regularity with these goats, and upon inquiry we found out the little fellows organized themselves into regular guards. They had a captain, quite a little fellow of dear old Billy Mein's (52nd Regiment); their time of duty was as regular as our soldiers': they had sentries with long white sticks in their hands, and Mein's little boy held a sort of court-martial, and would lick a boy awfully who neglected his charge.

My little boy's name was Antonio, and when he was for guard, I have seen him turn out unusually smart, with his face and hands washed. This little republic was very extraordinary, and quite true to the letter as I have drawn it. Mein's little captain told it all to my wife, who took great interest in them after she was acquainted with their organization, and the captain often consulted her. When our army was broken up after Toulouse, and all the Portuguese Corps of course marched back into Portugal, and the followers with them, we all of us gave our goats to the poor little boys to whom we had been so much indebted. My little fellow had a flock of fifteen. Many are probably great goat-proprietors now from this basis for future fortune.

Our Brigade was now commanded by Colonel Colborne, in whom we all had the most implicit confidence. I looked up to him as a man whose regard I hoped to deserve, and by whose knowledge and experience I desired to profit. He had more knowledge of ground, better understood the posting of picquets, consequently required fewer men on duty (he always strengthened every post by throwing obstacles -- trees, stones, carts, etc. -- on the road, to prevent a rush at night), knew better what the enemy were going to do, and more quickly anticipated his design than any officer; with that coolness and animation, under fire, no matter how hot, which marks a good huntsman when he finds his fox in his best country.

The French were now erecting works, upon a position by nature strong as one could well devise, for the purpose of defending the Pass of Vera, and every day Colonel Colborne and I took rides to look at them, with a pleasant reflexion that the stronger the works were, the greater the difficulty we should have in turning them out -- an achievement we well knew in store for us. On Oct. 7, the Duke resolved to cross the Bidassoa, and push the enemy at once into his own country, San Sebastian having been taken. Now had arrived the time we long had anticipated of a regular tussle with our fortified friends on the heights of Vera.

On the afternoon of the 7th, about two o'clock, we were formed for the attack, and so soon as the head of the 4th Division under that noble fellow, Sir Lowry Cole, appeared in sight, we received the command to move forward. We attacked on three different points. Advancing to the attack, Colborne, who had taken a liking to me as an active fellow, says:

"Now, Smith, you see the heights above us?"

"Well," I said, "I wish we were there." He laughed.

"When we are," he says, "and you are not knocked over, you shall be a Brevet-Major, if my recommendation has any weight at head-quarters." Backed by the performance of our Brigade, next day off he posted to Lord Fitzroy Somerset, and came back as happy as a soldier ever is who serves his comrade.

"Well, Major Smith, give me your hand." I did, and my heart too. Kind-hearted Colonel Barnard heard of this, went to Lord Fitzroy Somerset, asking for the Brevet for one of his Captains, remarking that I should be made a Major over the heads of twenty in my own Regiment. This startling fact obliged Lord Fitzroy to lay the matter before the Duke, who, I am told, said:

"A pity, by G—! Colborne and the Brigade are so anxious about it, and he deserves anything. If Smith will go and serve as Brigade-Major to another Brigade, I will give him the rank after the next battle."

Colborne's mortification was so great that I banished mine altogether by way of alleviating his disappointment. There was such a demonstration of justice on the part of his Grace, and so did I love the fellows whose heads I should have jumped over, that, honestly and truly, I soon forgot the affair. Colborne said:

"Go and serve with another Brigade."

"No," says I, "dear Colonel, not to be made of your rank. Here I will fight on happily, daily acquiring knowledge from your ability."

The 1st Caçadores, under poor Colonel Algeo, moved so as to threaten the enemy's left, and intercept or harass the retreat of the troops in the redoubt (which the noble 52nd were destined to carry at the point of the bayonet without one check), and the 2nd Battalion of the 95th and the 3rd Caçadores moved to the enemy's right of this redoubt for a similar purpose. This Battalion was fiercely opposed, but so soon as it succeeded in putting back the enemy, Colonel Colborne, at the head of the 52nd, with an eye like a hawk's, saw the moment had arrived, and he gave the word "Forward." One rush put us in possession of the redoubt, and the Caçadores and 2nd Battalion 95th caused the enemy great loss in his retreat to the top of the pass where his great defence was made. The redoubt just carried was placed on the ridge of the ravine, and must be carried ere any advance could be made on the actual position.

In this attack poor Algeo was killed. He rode a chestnut horse marked precisely as my celebrated hunter and war-horse, "Old Chap," which I rode on that day. My wife was looking on the fight from the very cottage window we had occupied so long, barely without the range of musketry, and saw this horse gallop to the rear, dragging for some distance the body by the stirrup. The impulse of the moment caused her with one shriek to rush towards it, and so did anxiety and fright add to her speed that my servant for some time could not overtake her. The horse came on, when she soon recognized it was poor Algeo's charger, not mine, and fell senseless from emotion, but soon recovered, to express her gratitude to Almighty God.

After this attack -- and there never was a more brilliant one -- the 4th Division was well pushed up the hill, and, so soon as our Brigade was reformed, we prepared for the great struggle on the top of the Pass of Vera. Colborne sent me to Sir Lowry to tell him what he was about to attempt, and to express his hope of a support to what he had just so vigorously commenced.

General Cole was all animation, and said, "Rely on my support, and you will need it, for you have a tough struggle before you."

On my return, we again advanced with a swarm of Riflemen in skirmishing order keeping up a murderous fire. Firing up a hill is far more destructive than firing down, as the balls in the latter case fly over. The 52nd Regiment, well in hand, with their bayonets sharp and glistening in the sun (for the afternoon was beautiful), were advanced under a most heavy fire, but, from the cause mentioned, it was not near so destructive as we expected. Still more to our astonishment, the enemy did not defend their well-constructed work as determinedly as we anticipated. Although they stood behind their parapets until we were in the act of leaping on them, they then gave way, and we were almost mixed together, till they precipitated themselves into a ravine, and fled down almost out of sight as if by magic.

On the opposite side of this ravine, a few of the Riflemen of General Kempt's Brigade were pushing forward with a noble fellow, Reid, of the Engineers, at their head. At the moment he did not know how full of the enemy the ravine was. Colonel Colborne and I were on horseback. We pushed on, a little madly, I admit, followed by those who could run fastest, until the ravine expanded and a whole column of French were visible, but we and Reid on the opposite side were rather ahead, while the enemy could not see from out the ravine. The few men who were there could not have resisted them, and certainly could not have cut them off; had they been aware.

Colonel Colborne, however, galloped up to the officer at the head of the column with the bearing of a man supported by

10,000, and said to the officer in French, "You are cut off. Lay down your arms."

The officer, a fine soldier-like looking fellow, as cool as possible, says, presenting his sword to Colonel Colborne, "There, Monsieur, is a sword which has ever done its duty," and then ordered his men to lay down their arms.

Colborne, with the presence of mind which stamps the character of a soldier, said, "Face your men to the left, and move out of the ravine." By this means the French Soldiers were separated from their arms.

At this moment there were up with Colborne myself; Winterbottom, Adjutant of the 52nd Regiment, my brother Tom, Adjutant of the 95th, and probably ten soldiers, and about as many with Reid on the opposite ridge. Reid wisely did not halt, but pushed forward, which added to the Frenchman's impression of our numbers, and Colborne turns to me, "Quick, Smith; what do you here? Get a few men together, or we are yet in a scrape."

The French having moved from their arms, Colborne desired the officer commanding to order them to sit down. Our men were rapidly coming up and forming, and, when our strength permitted, we ordered the enemy to march out of the ravine, and there were 22 officers and 400 men. Three pieces of cannon we had previously carried. Colonel Colborne, myself, and others were called madmen for our audacity. I never witnessed such presence of mind as Colborne evinced on this occasion, and when, like a man as he is, he returned the poor Frenchman's sword, "There," he says, "wear the sword, your pride; it is not yet disgraced." The fortune of war gave us the advantage over equal bravery.

By this time our men had got well out of the Pyrenees into the plain of France below, and as night was rapidly approaching, I was sent on to halt them, ready for Colonel Colborne to take up his position. The prisoners were sent to the rear (what became of their arms I never knew) under charge of a Lieutenant Cargill, of the 52nd Regiment, a manly, rough young subaltern, who on his march, just at dusk, met the Duke, who says, "Halloa, sir, where did you get those fellows?"

"In France. Colonel Colborne's Brigade took them."

"How the devil do you know it was France?"

"Because I saw a lot of our fellows coming into the column just before I left with pigs and poultry, which we had not on the Spanish side." The Duke turned hastily away without saying a word.

The next morning Mr. Cargill reported this to Colonel Colborne, whom I hardly ever saw so angry.

"Why, Mr. Cargill, you were not such a blockhead as to tell the Duke that, were you?"

In very broad Scotch, "What for no? It was fact as death."

It did not escape the Duke, who spoke to Colborne, saying, "Though your Brigade have even more than usually distinguished themselves, we must respect the property of the country."

"I am fully aware of it, my lord, and can rely upon the discipline of my soldiers, but your lordship well knows in the very heat of action a little irregularity will occur."

"Ah, ah!" says my lord, "stop it in future, Colborne." Nor had his Grace cause to complain of us.

This night we slept on our arms, and cold and miserable we were, for no baggage had been permitted to come to us. The next day we occupied the heights of Vera, our outposts remaining pushed forward, and head-quarters and our general hospital were established at Vera. My wife joined me very early, and I never before had seen her under such excitement, the effect of the previous day, when, as she conceived at the moment, she had seen me killed. She did not recover her usual vivacity for several days. We remained in this position several days.

One day I dressed myself in all my best to do a little dandy at head-quarters, to see some of my wounded comrades and officers, and to look into our hospitals. In galloping through the country, I heard a very melancholy and faint call, repeated once or twice without attracting my attention. When I turned towards it, it was repeated. I rode up and among several dead bodies of the enemy, I found the poor fellow who had called to me greatly exhausted. Four days had elapsed since the action, and he had both legs shot off high up. I dismounted and felt his pulse, which was still far from faint. Of course he prayed me to send succour. I promised to do so, and I proceeded to tie some of the bushes of the underwood to mark the spot, and continued to do so until I reached a mountain track leading to Vera. I now even hear the hideous moans he uttered when I turned from him, although I earnestly assured him of help. Away I galloped to the hospital, not to visit my own poor fellows, but to get a fatigue party and a stretcher, and off I set for my poor wounded enemy, whom, from the precautions taken, I easily found.

Poor thing, from the belief that I had abandoned him, he was nearly exhausted. We got him on the stretcher, the party set off to the hospital, and I to my bivouac, for it was late and I was well aware the poor thing would be treated just as one of our own soldiers. I had literally forgotten the circumstance, when one day after we had advanced considerably into France, a month or five weeks after the man was picked up, a large convoy of disabled men, as an act of humanity, were sent to their own country from the rear. My Brigade was of course on the outpost, and it became my duty to go to the enemy's advanced post close to, with a letter and flag of truce. I was received as usual with great civility, and the convoy passed on. While I was talking to the French officers, a poor fellow on one of the stretchers called to me and the officer, and began a volley of thanks, which, if it had been of musquetry, would have been difficult to resist. I said:

"I know nothing about you, poor fellow; that will do."

"I know you; I owe my life to you; you fetched the party who carried me to hospital. Both stumps were amputated; I am now doing perfectly well, and I was treated like one of your own soldiers." I never saw gratitude so forcibly expressed in my life.

Chapter 15

Campaign of 1813 -- Battle of Nivelle

Our Division was soon after pushed forward to our right on a ridge somewhat in advance, and fully looking upon the enemy's position. His right extended from St. Jean de Luz, his left was on the Nivelle, his centre on La Petite Rhune and the heights beyond that village. Our Division was in the very centre opposite La Petite Rhune.

One morning Colonel Colborne and I were at the advance vedette at daylight, and saw a French picquet of an officer and fifty men come down to occupy a piece of rising ground between our respective advanced posts, as to which the night before I and a French staff-officer had agreed that neither should put a picquet on it. (Such arrangements were very commonly made.) Colonel Colborne said:

"Gallop up to the officer, wave him back, or tell him he shall not put a picquet there."

Having waved to no purpose, I then rode towards him and called to him. He still moved on, so I galloped back. Colborne fell in our picquet, ordered up a reserve, and fired five or six shots over the heads of the Frenchmen. They then went back immediately, and the hill became, as previously agreed, neutral ground. I give this anecdote to show how gentleman-like enemies of disciplined armies can be; there was no such courtesy between French and Spaniards.

A few days previously to Nov. 10, the Battle of the Nivelle, the Division took ground on the ridge of hills in our occupation, and the extreme right of the Division became the left. Gilmour, commanding the 1st Battalion of the Rifles, then in the 1st Brigade, had built a very nice little mud hut about ten feet square with a chimney, fireplace, and a door made of wattle and a bullock's hide. When my wife rode up, Gilmour had just turned out.

The night was bitterly cold; it was November in the Pyrenees. Gilmour says:

"Jump off and come into your own castle, which I in perpetuity bequeath to you."

When I returned from my Brigade and new line of picquets, etc., I found my wife as warm and as snug as possible -- dinner prepared for me and Tom Fane, our horses all bivouacked, our cold tent pitched, and our servants established in it; all was comfort, happiness, and joy, every want supplied, every care banished. At night we retired to our nuptial couch, a hard mattress on the floor, when a sudden storm of rain came on. In ten seconds it came down through the roof of our black-earth sods, and, literally in a moment, we were drenched to the skin and as black as chimney-sweepers. The buoyant spirits of my wife, and the ridiculous position we were in, made her laugh herself warm. We turned the servants out of our tent, and never enjoyed the late comforts of our castle again.

The enemy, not considering this ground strong enough, turned to it with a vigour I have rarely witnessed, to fortify it by every means art could devise. Every day, before the position was attacked, Colonel Colborne and I went to look at their progress; the Duke himself would come to our outpost, and continue walking there a long time.

One day he stayed unusually long. He turns to Colborne, "These fellows think themselves invulnerable, but I will beat them out, and with great ease."

"That we shall beat them," says Colborne, "when your lordship attacks, I have no doubt, but for the ease -- "

"Ah, Colborne, with your local knowledge only, you are perfectly right; it appears difficult, but the enemy have not men to man the works and lines they occupy. They dare not concentrate a sufficient body to resist the attacks I shall make upon them. I can pour a greater force on certain points than they can concentrate to resist me."

"Now I see it, my lord," says Colborne.

The Duke was lying down, and began a very earnest conversation. General Alten, Kempt, Colborne, I, and other staff-officers were preparing to leave the Duke, when he says:

"Oh, lie still." After he had conversed for some time with Sir G. Murray, Murray took out of his sabretache his writing-materials, and began to write the plan of attack for the whole army.

When it was finished, so clearly had he understood the Duke, I do not think he erased one word. He says, "My lord, is this your desire?" It was one of the most interesting scenes I have ever witnessed. As Murray read, the Duke's eye was directed with his telescope to the spot in question. He never asked Sir G. Murray one question, but the muscles of his face evinced lines of the deepest thought.

When Sir G. Murray had finished, the Duke smiled and said, "Ah, Murray, this will put us in possession of the fellows' lines. Shall we be ready to-morrow?"

"I fear not, my lord, but next day."

"Now, Alten," says the Duke, "if, during the night previous to the attack, the Light Division could be formed on this very ground, so as to rush at La Petite Rhune just as day dawned, it would be of vast importance and save great loss, and by thus precipitating yourselves on the right of the works of La Petite Rhune, you would certainly carry them." This Petite Rhune was well occupied both by men and works, and a tough affair was in prospect.

General Alten says, "I 'dink' I can, my lord."

Kempt says, "My Brigade has a road. There can be no difficulty, my lord."

Colborne says, "For me there is no road, but Smith and I both know every bush and every stone. We have studied what we have daily expected, and in the darkest night we can lead the Brigade to this very spot." I was proud enough at thus being associated, but no credit was due to me. "Depend on me, my lord," says Colborne.

"Well then, Alten, when you receive your orders as to the attack, let it be so."

Just before starting on this night's march, [9 Nov.], having had many military arrangements to make before I got on my horse, I had got a short distance when I remarked that, although I knew a proper tough fight was in hand, I had forgotten to bid my "good-bye" to my wife, which habit (on my part, at least) had rendered about as formal as if going to London out of the country. Her feelings were acute enough on such occasions, so I went into my hut, and avowed my neglect.

She looked very sad, and I said, "Hallo, what's the matter?"

"You or your horse will be killed to-morrow."

I laughed and said, "Well, of two such chances, I hope it may be the horse." We parted, but she was very sad indeed.

As we started for our position before the great, the important day [Battle of Nivelle, 10 Nov.], the night was very dark. We had no road, and positively nothing to guide us but knowing the bushes and stones over a mountain ridge.

Colborne stayed near the Brigade, and sent me on from spot to spot which we both knew, when he would come up to me and satisfy himself that I was right. I then went on again. In this manner we crept up with our Brigade to our advanced picquet within a hundred and fifty yards of the enemy.

We afterwards found Kempt's Brigade close to our right, equally successfully posted. When Colborne and I rode up to our most advanced picquet, of course by the rear, we found, to the delight of us both, the Sergeant, Crowther, and his men, all sitting round a fire, as alert as if on sentry themselves, with their rifles between their legs, the sentry a few paces in their front. We had crept up by ourselves. Without any agitation, they stood up very quietly to reconnoitre us, when Colborne spoke, and commended their vigilance.

I and Tom Fane, Skerrett's A.D.C., who nobly stayed with me rather than go to the rear, lay down for about two hours, when I could sleep, but Tom told me he could not. He had had a small flask of brandy, but, what with the cold and the necessity of keeping it out, the brandy was exhausted.

About an hour before daylight, by some accident, a soldier's musket went off. It was a most anxious moment, for we thought the enemy had discovered us, and, if they had not, such shots might be repeated, and they would; but most fortunately all was still. I never saw Colborne so excited as he was for the moment.

The anxious moment of appearing day arrived. We fell in, and our attack was made on the enemy's position in seven columns, nor did we ever meet a check, but carried the enemy's works, the tents all standing, by one fell swoop of irresistible victory. Napier, at the head of the 43rd, had his pantaloons torn by the ball, and singed by the fire, of one of the enemy from the parapet of their works. Such was the attack and such the resistance, that a few prisoners whom we took declared that they and their officers were perfectly thunderstruck, for they had no conception any force was near them. The 4th Division had some heavy fighting on our right. Ours was the most beautiful attack ever made in the history of war.

The key of the enemy's position was in our hands, and the great line was our next immediate object. We were speedily reformed, and ready for our attack on the enemy's line-position and strong field fortifications. In descending La Petite Rhune, we were much exposed to the enemy's fire, and when we got to the foot of the hill we were about to attack, we had to cross a road enfiladed very judiciously by the enemy, which caused some loss. We promptly stormed the enemy's works and as promptly carried them.

I never saw our men fight with such lively pluck; they were irresistible; and we saw the other Divisions equally successful, the enemy flying in every direction. Our Riflemen were pressing them in their own style, for the French themselves are terrific in pursuit, when poor dear gallant (Sir Andrew) Barnard was knocked off his horse by a musket-ball through his lungs. When Johnny Kincaid, his adjutant, got up to him, he was nearly choked by blood in his mouth. They washed it out for him, and he recovered so as to give particular orders about a pocket-book and some papers he wished sent to his brother. He did not want assistance; the soldiers loved him; he was borne off to the rear, and, when examined by Assistant-Surgeon Robson, it was found that the ball had not passed through, but was perceptible to the touch.

The surgeon had him held up, so that when he made a bold incision to let the ball out, its own weight would prevent its being repelled into the cavity of the chest. The ball was boldly and judiciously extracted, no fever came on, and in three weeks Barnard was at the head of a Brigade, with one wound still open, and in the passage of the Gave d'Oleron he plunged into the water, and saved the life of a soldier floating down the river.

But to the fight. Everything was carried apparently, and our

Division was halted. Some sharp skirmishing was going on, and Colborne and I were standing with the 52nd Regiment, again ready for anything, on a neck of land which conducted to a strong-looking star redoubt, the only work the enemy still held, when Charlie Beckwith, the A.Q.M.G. of our Division, came up with orders from General Alten to move on.

"What, Charlie, to attack that redoubt? Why, if we leave it to our right or left, it must fall, as a matter of course; our whole army will be beyond it in twenty minutes."

"I don't know; your orders are to move on."

"Am I to attack the redoubt?" says Colborne.

"Your orders are to move on," and off he galloped.

Colborne turns to me, and says, "What an evasive order!"

"Oh, sir," says I, "let us take the last of their works; it will be the operation of a few minutes," and on we went in a column of companies.

As we neared the enemy, Colborne's brilliant eye saw they were going to hold it, for it was a closed work, and he says, "Smith, they do not mean to go until fairly driven out; come, let us get off our horses."

I was just mounted on a beautiful thoroughbred mare, my "Old Chap" horse being somewhat done, and I really believed anything like fighting was all over. I said nothing, but sat still, and on we went with a hurrah which we meant should succeed, but which the garrison intended should do no such thing. My horse was struck within twenty yards of the ditch, and I turned her round so that I might jump off, placing her between me and the fire, which was very hot. As I was jumping off, another shot struck her, and she fell upon me with a crash, which I thought had squeezed me as flat as a thread-paper, her blood, like a fountain, pouring into my face.

The 52nd were not beat back, but swerved from the redoubt into a ravine, for they could not carry it. While lying under my horse, I saw one of the enemy jump on the parapet of the works in an undaunted manner and in defiance of our attack, when suddenly he started straight up into the air, really a considerable height, and fell headlong into the ditch. A ball had struck him in the forehead,

I suppose — the fire of our skirmishers was very heavy on the redoubt. Our whole army was actually passing to the rear of the redoubt. Colborne, in the most gallant manner, jumped on his horse, rode up to the ditch under the fire of the enemy, which, however, slackened as he loudly summoned the garrison to surrender.

The French officer, equally plucky, said, "Retire, sir, or I will shoot you!" Colborne deliberately addressed the men.

"If a shot is fired, now that you are surrounded by our army, we will put every man to the sword."

By this time I succeeded in getting some soldiers, by calling to them, to drag me from under my horse, when they exclaimed, "Well, d— my eyes if our old Brigade-Major is killed, after all."

"Come, pull away," I said; "I am not even wounded, only squeezed."

"Why, you are as bloody as a butcher."

I ran to Colborne just as he had finished his speech. He took a little bit of paper out, wrote on it, "I surrender unconditionally," and gave it to me to give the French officer, who laughed at the state of blood I was in. He signed it, and Colborne sent me to the Duke.

When I rode up (on a horse just lent me), his Grace says, "Who are you?"

"The Brigade-Major, 2nd Rifle Brigade."

"Hullo, Smith, are you badly wounded?"

"Not at all, sir; it is my horse's blood."

"Well." I gave him the paper. "Tell Colborne I approve."

The garrison began to march out just as my Brigade were again moved on, and General Downie was left to receive it with his Spaniards. The garrison was composed of the whole of the French 88th Regiment, complete in every respect. The Duke was sorry we had attacked, for the 52nd lost many men, and it never was the Duke's intention, as he saw what Colborne had previously observed. Some discussion afterwards took place as to the order Colborne received. However, I think now, as I did then, move on implied attack.

This was a most brilliant day's fighting, and showed how irresistible our army was. As the Duke foretold, the enemy had not men enough. We were never opposed to a formed body. The whole army was in occupation of their works, and when we penetrated, retired. A proclamation had been issued to show the French inhabitants we made war on their army, not on them, and never in an enemy's country was such rigid discipline maintained as by the British Army. It is scarcely to be credited. The day after the battle our baggage moved up, and my wife joined me, horror-struck at the state of my cocked hat, clothes, and only half-washed face. She would not believe I was not awfully wounded, and then reminded me of her prophecy, that either I or my horse would be killed the following day.

A curious coincidence occurred in respect to this horse. Shortly before the Battle of Salamanca [22 July, 1812] a great friend of mine, Lindsay, of the 11th Dragoons, came and prayed me to take it in exchange for a magnificent brown mare I had bought from Charlie Rowan; he had often tempted me, but I resisted, but upon this occasion I yielded, so earnest was he for a Dragoon's charger; and he gave me sixty guineas to boot. In a few months he was killed off my gallant mare on the Bridge of Tudela on the Douro, and now his mare was killed under me as described. Lord Fitzroy Somerset bought his mare at the sale; his lordship afterwards sold her to me, and she went with me to Washington. I brought her back, gave her to a brother, and she bred many foals afterwards.

Chapter 16

Combat of the 10th December -- Harry Smith's Dream, and the Death of His Mother

The following day we moved into a most beautiful country, intersected with hedgerows, and the finest and sweetest second crop of hay I ever saw, which our horses rejoiced in. We took up our posts in front of Arbonne [15 Nov.], and the following day had a sharp skirmish at our advanced posts. We halted here a day or two, and then moved on to a line more approaching Bayonne. The first Brigade occupied the Chateau d'Arcangues [17 Nov.]; the second the Chateau of Castilleur, where Colonel Colborne packed the 52nd Regiment as close as cards; and the 2nd Battalion, 95th Regiment, and the 1st and 3rd Caçadores also had cover. Our posts were here very close upon each other, and we had far more skirmishing and alarms than usual.

Upon the morning of the 9th December, the 1st and 7th Divisions came close up to our rear, which led us to suppose something was going on. The enemy in our front were alarmed, and stood to their arms. Shortly after these Divisions moved to our right, for the purpose of crossing the river [Nive], and our Division moved on to drive back the enemy's picquets in the direction of Bayonne. To occupy his attention, our Riflemen formed up before the firing commenced close to the enemy's strongest post, on the high-road to Bayonne, where we had been watching each other for several days. When I and Beckwith, the A.Q.M.G., rode up and ordered our people to advance, not a shot was fired. The French saw we were going to attack, but did not withdraw their picquet. We beckoned to them to do so, but they would not take the hint. We then actually fired some shots over their heads. There was positively a reluctance on our part to shoot any man in so cold-blooded a manner. The moment a shot was fired the affair became general, and we drove in the French picquets, who rapidly retired, and we had little fighting all day. In the evening, having effected the demonstration required, the Division retired to its old ground, and we resumed our usual line of picquets.

On the following morning [10 Dec.], having a presentiment the enemy would create a considerable diversion upon the left of our army, I was with our most advanced picquets before daylight. I had not been there many minutes, when I was joined by Beckwith, and soon after up came Colborne.

We said, "The enemy are going to attack us."

Colborne said, "No; they are only going to resume their ordinary posts in our front."

I said, "But look at the body in our immediate front, and a column far off; evidently moving on the 1st Division," which was on the extreme left. It was evident we should be attacked immediately, and I said so, but Colborne asserted it was no such thing. I prayed him to allow me to order my Brigade under arms.

At last he consented, and, although I rode at the utmost speed, our troops were barely out in time, so furiously did the French drive us back. They took the Chateau of Castilleur from us, making at the same time a heavy attack on that of Arcangues. Much of our baggage fell into the enemy's hands, although they could not carry it off. My wife had barely time to slip on her habit and jump upon her horse; her Vittoria pug-dog in the scuffle was left behind, so sharp was the fire on the Chateau. A bugler of the 52nd Regiment, however, knew the pug, whipped him up, and put him in his haversack. This was nearer a surprise than anything we had ever experienced. For some time the enemy possessed our quarters and bivouac, and -- what was of great importance to Tom Fane -- rifled his portmanteau. They also carried off a goose which was fattening for our Christmas dinner. We soon repaid our friends with interest and retook our position, but it was one of as heavy attacks as I have ever witnessed.

In the afternoon of that day, the enemy made a most vigorous attack on Sir J. Hope, particularly at the Mayor's House of Biaritz, sharply skirmishing with us at the same time to occupy our attention. I thought then, and I think now, if my Brigade had been moved on the left of the attack on Sir J. Hope, it would have caused the enemy great loss, as his flank was exposed, but the Duke of Wellington knew better, and never attempted hazardous and little affairs, but ever played a great and safe game.

That evening the Regiments of Nassau and Frankfort walked over to us from the French lines into those of the 7th Division at Arbonne. Colonel Beyring, Count Alten's A.D.C., was said to have been for some time with them, and it was evident the Duke knew about their intention.

Upon the 11th [Dec.] we had some partial skirmishing. The 2nd Battalion Rifle Brigade struck their tents for the purpose of moving their ground. The enemy were most alarmed, and took up their ground to receive us. That night, when our armies were dismissed, rations were served out. In my life I never heard such a row as among the French when preparing to cook. I was posting the night's sentries, when I saw a French officer doing the same. I went towards him, and we civilly greeted each other. I said I wished to speak to him. He came up with the greatest confidence and good humour. I showed him my vedette, and then remarked that his was too far in advance and might create an alarm at night when relieving. He said he did not see that, but to please me, if I would point out where I wished he should be, he would immediately move him -- which he did. He presented his little flask of excellent French brandy, of which I took a sup, and we parted in perfect amity.

When I returned to Colborne, who was in the Chateau, I found him lying asleep before a fire just as he had got off his horse. I did not awake him, nor had I anything to eat. Sleep at night readily supplies the place of food, and hunger at night on that account is not nearly so acute and painful as in the morning, when your day's work is before you. Down I lay, without one thought in the world, from exhaustion. I had a long dream, its purport that the enemy had attacked my father's house (the front of which opened to the street, the back into a beautiful garden, by what we children called "The Black Door"). My father had my mother in his arms; I saw them as plainly as ever I did in my life, he carrying her through the Black Door, at the moment calling out, "Now, some one shut the door; she is safe and rescued."

At the instant I sprang on my feet, and in our usual military words in cases of alarm, roared out in a voice of thunder, "Stand to your arms." Colborne was on his feet like a shot, the light of the fire showed me the room and my delusion, and I said, "Oh, sir, I beg your pardon; I have been dreaming."

He said, in his noble way, "Never mind, it is near daylight, and it shows that asleep or awake, you are intent on your duty." He lay down, and was asleep in a moment.

I never felt so oppressed in my life, so vividly was depicted to my mind the scene described, and I took out of my pocket a little roster of duties and picquets bound in calf-skin, and noted down the hour and particulars of my dream. In a few days I received a letter from my afflicted father, telling me my mother died on Sunday morning, Dec. 12, at one o'clock, at the very moment I cried out, "Stand to your arms." Such is the fact. When I lay down, I was tired and exhausted, as before expressed. I had not a thought in the world of home or anything, nor was I prepared for the probability of the event. I presume to make no remarks on such intimations from God alone, but the whole day I was heavy and oppressed, nor did I ever shake off the vivid impression until the receipt of the letter put me in possession of the loss I had sustained.

Her dying moments were perfectly composed; to the last she blessed her two sons engaged in the wars of their country, and died saying, "Would I could have seen them after their dangers and good conduct!"

The morning after my dream [12 Dec.] I was very early at our advanced posts, and I saw some French soldiers coming on in a very unusual manner to attack us, while the mass of their force were dismissed in bivouac. The 1st Caçadores had the advance. I never saw the French so daring since the retreat to Coruña, and they were most excellent shots, and actually astonished our Caçadores. Colborne, hearing a smart firing, rode up, and stopped in the road opposite one of the barricades of our picquets.

I said, "I don't know what the devil we have got in our front today. Don't stand there, you will be shot in a moment!" He laughed, but would not move. In a second a ball went through his cap just above his noble head. He moved then and laughed.

"Look at the fellows," he says, "how viciously they come on; it is evident it is no general attack, for the troops in their bivouac are not under arms. They want this post."

"Which," says I, "they will have in ten minutes, unless I bring up the 2nd Battalion Rifle Brigade," for our Caçadores were evidently not equal to their task.

Colborne says, "Fetch them!"

In a very short time our Riflemen came up. By this time the enemy had driven in everything beyond the barricade, and were prepared to assault it. Our 95th fellows had a few men wounded as they were coming up the road, before they could be extended, which made them as savage as the enemy, who were capering about the fields in our front as if drunk. Our fellows turned to, and soon brought them to repent any pranks or exposure. We took a few prisoners, and ascertained the Regiment was the 32nd Voltigeurs, a crack corps of Suchet's army which had joined the night before, when we heard all the noise going on in the bivouac. These gentlemen had ever previously been venturous and laughed at the tales of British prowess; that morning's lesson, however, seemed to have made converts of them, for I never after observed any extra feats of dancing; but Colborne and all of us were perfectly astonished when the fact was known, and our 2nd Battalion 95th Regiment were rather elated in having thus shown themselves such able instructors.

We were very much on the alert all day, and a few shots were exchanged. At night our picquets were strengthened, for we were not aware if our friends, the new Voltigeurs, intended a fresh prank. After these three days' fighting and vigilance, the enemy withdrew close to Bayonne, their and our advanced posts being nearly as before. Notwithstanding the loss of our goose, we had a capital Christmas dinner, at which, of course, we had the Commissary of the Brigade, and induced him to find us champagne, which many commissaries were able to do.

Chapter 17

Campaign of 1814 -- Battle of Orthez -- Anecdote of Juana Smith

From the Chateau of Castilleur we moved more into the mountains to the rear and to our left of Ustaritz, where we never saw the enemy [Jan. 1814]. Our time was spent in shooting, and exploring the mountains. While we were in this position forage was very scarce, and we chopped up the furze-bushes very small by way of hay. It is astonishing how it agreed with the horses. The natives use it in the same way for their cattle.

We remained in this position until the end of February, when we moved, reaching Orthez on the 26th. Here our Division had one of the sharpest skirmishes in a town which I ever saw. Orthez is situated on both sides of the Gave de Pau and has a bridge, which the enemy held with great jealousy. On the afternoon of this day, the Duke and his head-quarters came up. It was his intention to have fought the battle that afternoon, had the 3rd Division been able to reach its position in time.

I heard the Duke say, "Very well, Murray, if the Division does not arrive in time, we must delay the attack till to-morrow. However, I must have a sleep." He folded his little white cloak round him, and lay down, saying, "Call me in time, Murray."

Murray awoke the Duke, saying, "It is too late to-day, my Lord."

"Very well, then, my orders for to-morrow hold good."

At dark we withdrew all our posts out of Orthez but a picquet near the bridge in the town, and at daylight [27 Feb.] we crossed by a pontoon bridge below Orthez, and marched over difficult ground. We saw the enemy very strongly posted, both as regards the elevation and the nature of the ground, which was intersected by large banks and ditches, while the fences of the field were most admirably calculated for vigorous defence. As we were moving on the right of the 3rd Division, Sir Thomas Picton, who was ever ready to find fault with the Light, rode up to Colonel Barnard.

"Who the devil are you?" knowing Barnard intimately.

"We are the Light Division."

"If you are Light, sir, I wish you would move a little quicker," said in his most bitter and sarcastic tone.

Barnard says very cool, "Alten commands. But the march of infantry is quick time, and you cannot accelerate the pace of the head of the column without doing an injury to the whole. Wherever the 3rd Division are, Sir Thomas, we will be in our places, depend on it."

We were soon engaged, but less for some time than the troops to our right and left. I never saw the French fight so hard as this day, and we were actually making no advance, when the Duke came up, and ordered the 52nd Regiment to form line and advance. The Battalion was upwards of seven hundred strong. It deployed into line like clockwork, and moved on, supported by clouds of sharpshooters. It was the most majestic advance I ever saw. The French, seeing this line advance so steadily, were appalled; their fire, which at first was terrific, gradually decreased as we neared. The Divisions on our right and left also moved on. The battle was won.

In this advance the 52nd suffered considerably. The present Duke of Richmond, then Lord March, a Captain in the corps, received a severe wound in the side; the ball still annoys him. The Duke himself also got a crack on his knee, which lamed him for several days. When Lord March lay on the ground after the attack, I went to bring up Maling, Surgeon of the 52nd Regiment. As soon as he arrived, to my horror, he poked his forefinger into the wound to trace the course of the ball. At this moment up rode Lord Fitzroy Somerset, and Lord March's brother, Lord George Lennox, awfully affected, believing the wound mortal.

Lord March said, "Maling, tell me if I am mortally wounded, because I have something I wish to impart to George."

Maling said, "If you will be quiet, you will do very well." Maling did not think so. However, Lord March made a miraculous recovery. I never knew a finer young fellow, braver or cooler. In those days, he would not have opposed his kind patron, the Duke, as he did subsequently. That every peer and every other man should speak out his mind according to his conscience, I earnestly desire;

but, as Duke of Richmond, he opposed the Duke of Wellington politically in a manner rather partaking of personal hostility than political consistency. Every admirer of Lord March in the army, and he had many, lamented the course he pursued.

But to the fight. We drove the enemy in great confusion before us. On this occasion, I literally lost a Battalion of my Brigade, the 1st Caçadores, for two days, they got so mixed with the 6th Division. The night I found them, after much diligence, I and my Brigadier, Barnard, got into a little sort of inn, kept by an old soldier disabled in Bonaparte's Italian campaigns. He did not require to be told the wants of a soldier, but from habit and sympathy turned to like a "good 'un" to cook us some dinner.

As he was hard at work, he said to Barnard, "Ah, the French are not always victorious, and I see war now is [not?] what it was when I served. The Cavalry give way first, then come the Artillery, and then follow the Infantry in disorder."

He became in the course of the evening very eloquent over his own wine, and told us some very amusing stories. The next morning, when Barnard paid him for everything we had consumed, he was perfectly thunderstruck. I shall never forget his astonishment or his "Eh bien! monsieur, comme vous voulez."

The baggage reached us early the following day [1 March], and in the afternoon we forded the Adour, which was deep, rapid, and broad. My wife had ridden over the field of battle, and described it as covered with dead, dying, and wounded. She observed an extraordinary number of wounds in the head. These were due to the fact that, owing to the cover of the high banks before described, the head only was vulnerable or exposed. She saw one fine fellow of an Artilleryman with both his arms shot off, which he said occurred while he was ramming down the cartridge into his own gun. She offered him all she had in the eating or drinking way, but he most disdainfully refused all.

The same afternoon we made a long and rapid march on Mont de Marsan, where a Division of Cavalry and Marshal Beresford and his head-quarters preceded us. We did not reach Mont de Marsan until some hours after dark. We were ordered to take up quarters for the night, but so full of Cavalry and head-quarters was the place, and all scattered over the town, not collected, as we Light Division used to be by streets and regiments as if on parade, we had great difficulty in getting in anywhere.

The night was showery, with sleet drifting, frosty and excessively cold. My poor wife was almost perished. We at last got her into a comfortable little house, where the poor Frenchwoman, a widow, lighted a fire, and in about half an hour produced some bouillon in a very handsome Sèvres slop-basin, saying this had been a present to her many years ago on the day of her marriage, and that it had never been used since her husband's death. She, therefore, wished my wife to know how happy she was to wait on the nation who was freeing France of an usurper. The widow was a true "Royaliste," and we were both most grateful to the poor woman.

The next day we were ordered back to St. Sever, on the highroad to Toulouse, and parted with our widow with all mutual concern and gratitude, our baggage being left to follow. We had a very showery, frosty, and miserable long march over an execrable road, after which we and Barnard got into a little cottage on the roadside. At daylight the following morning we were expecting to move, but, having received no order, we turned to breakfast, my wife relating to Barnard the kindness she had received the previous night and the history of the basin. To our horror in came my servant, Joe Kitchen, with the identical slop-basin full of milk. The tears rolled down my wife's cheeks. Barnard got in a storming passion.

I said, "How dare you, sir, do anything of the sort?" (he was an excellent servant.)

"Lord, sir," he says, "why, the French soldiers would have carried off the widow, an' she had been young, and I thought it would be so nice for the goat's milk in the morning; she was very angry, though, 'cos I took it."

Barnard got on his horse, and rode to headquarters. About ten o'clock he came back and said the Duke told him the army would not march until to-morrow.

My wife immediately sent for the trusty groom, old West, and said, "Bring my horse and yours too, and a feed of corn in your haversack." She said to me, "I am going to see an officer who was wounded the day before yesterday, and if I am not back until late, do not be alarmed."

Young as she was, I never controlled her desire on such occasions, having perfect confidence in her superior sense and seeing her frequently visit our wounded or sick.

I went to my Brigade, having various duties, just before she started. It became dark, she had not returned, but Barnard would wait dinner for her, saying, "She will be in directly." She did arrive soon, very cold and splashed from hard riding on a very dirty, deep, and wet road.

She laughed and said, "Well, why did you wait dinner? Order it; I shall soon have my habit off."

Barnard and I exclaimed with one voice, "Where have you been?"

"Oh," she says, "do not be angry, I am not taken prisoner, as you see. I have been to Mont de Marsan, to take back the poor widow's basin." I never saw a warm-hearted fellow so delighted as Barnard.

"Well done, Juana, you are a heroine. The Maid of Saragossa is nothing to you."

She said the widow cried exceedingly with joy, but insisted on her now keeping the basin for the milk, which my wife would on no account do. She had ridden that day thirty miles and had every reason to expect to meet a French patrol.

I said, "Were you not afraid of being taken prisoner?"

"No, I and West kept a good look-out, and no French dragoon could catch me on my Spanish horse, Tiny." She was tired from the excessive cold, but the merit of her act sustained her as much as it inspired us with admiration.

The story soon got wind, and the next day every officer in the Division loaded her with praise. It was a kind and noble act which few men, much less a delicate girl of sixteen, would have done under all the circumstances. Our worthy friend, Bob Digby, of the 52nd Regiment, Barnard's A.D.C., overhearing my wife's orders to West, after she had started, most kindly followed and joined my wife on the road, for, as he said, he was alarmed lest she should fall in with a patrol.

Chapter 18

Campaign of 1814 -- At Gée, Near Aire -- Battle of Tarbes -- Battle of Tolouse -- End of the War

On our advance [9 March, etc.], we were for some days at a village called Gée, near Aire, where the 2nd Division, under Sir W. Stewart, had a brilliant little affair.

But I must first interpose an anecdote. One of his A.D.C.'s, his nephew, Lord Charles Spencer, a Lieutenant of the 95th Regiment, was mounted on a very valuable horse which he had paid more for than he could afford, contrary to the advice of Sir William. In driving the French through the town, Lord Charles's horse was shot on the bank of a large pond, into which he himself was thrown head foremost. (The fire at this moment was very heavy, and in a street more balls take effect than in the open.) Sir William very quietly says, "Ha, there goes my poor nephew and all his fortune," alluding to the price he paid for his horse.

I have often heard Colonel Colborne (Lord Seaton) affirm that if he were asked to name the bravest man he had ever seen (and no one was a better judge), he should name Sir William Stewart. Although he gave me my commission, I never saw him under fire. If he exceeded in bravery my dear friend, Sir Edward Pakenham, he was gallant indeed. Pakenham's bravery was of that animated, intrepid cast that he applied his mind vigorously at the moment to the position of his own troops as well as to that of the enemy, and by judicious foresight ensured success, but he never avoided a fight any sort.

The village of Gée was to the right of the high-road to Tolouse, the River [Adour] running to our right. The Cavalry were posted on the main road, their advance vedettes looking on to the village of [Tarsac?] where the enemy were very alert and obstinate in resisting our approach.

On the day the army advanced, the French Cavalry made a fierce resistance in the village, and when driven out, made some desperate charges on the chaussée, in one of which the officer in command was cut down while gallantly leading his Squadron. An officer of our 15th Hussars (I think Booth), having admired his gallant bearing, dismounted to his assistance. He said he believed he was not mortally wounded, and he requested to be carried to the Chateau in the village he had so gallantly fought for, where his father and family resided. This peculiar tale may be relied on, like everything else, as I hope, which I have asserted. For several days it was the usual topic of conversation, and when any one came from the rear, inquiry was always made if the French Captain who was wounded and in his father's house, (we never knew his name), was doing well. We learnt afterwards that he perfectly recovered, but the sword wound had stamped him with a deep scar.

At Gée we had several alerts, and our baggage for some successive days was loaded for hours. On one of these occasions the old housekeeper of a large house which Barnard occupied, and whom he had paid for many a fat fowl and fish out of tanks, etc., came into the room where my wife remained waiting to join the troops, seized my wife and vowed she would put her to death, grasping her with a fiend-like strength. Fortunately, at this moment my servant returned to say the Division were not to march, and rescued my poor affrighted and delicate wife. We afterwards learnt that this violent woman, if anything excited her, was afflicted with temporary insanity, and she had been put in a rage below, and came up to vent her spleen on my poor wife. We were in this house for two or three days after, but my wife had been so alarmed she would never allow her servant to quit her. The latter was a powerful woman of the 52nd, rejoicing in the name of Jenny Bates.

While in this village, Charlie Beckwith, the Q.M.G., came to me and said, "Harry, I want a Company for picquet immediately." I named the Corps, 1st Battalion 95th, who had one ready accoutred in waiting, as we always had in positions subject to alerts. It was out in five minutes, and Charlie Beckwith marched to point out where the officer commanding was to post it. I invariably went out with every picquet when possible. On this occasion I had other duty. In the afternoon I got on my horse to look for my picquet. I met Charlie Beckwith in the village.

He said, "I will ride with you." We did not find the picquet where we expected -- on our side of a bridge (beyond which was a comfortable village). Having heard no firing, we were not alarmed for the safety of the Company, still we could not find it.

We rode to the bridge, the object of the officer's watch, saying, "There will surely be a sentry upon it."

We rode up and found one certainly, but on the enemy's side. We asked where the Company was. The vedette was an Irishman.

"By Jasus, the Captain's the boy. It was so rainy and cold on the plain, he harboured us all comfortably, like the man that he is, in the village."

The French were in the habit of patrolling into this village in force, and, although the Captain had so posted himself as I do believe he would have been able to hold his own until the Division came up, it could have cost us a fight to rescue him from the far side of the bridge, which he ought never to have crossed. So the Captain got a blowing-up, and the Company had to make their fires in a cold, wet, and miserable bivouac. I never had a picquet out from the Brigade without visiting it so as to judge how it was posted, and how to withdraw it either at night or in case of abrupt necessity.

We had also a sharp skirmish at Vic Begorre, but the brunt of it fell on the 3rd Division, where one of the most able officers got himself killed where he had no business to be -- Major Sturgeon, of the Staff. I hold nothing to be more unsoldierlike than for officers well mounted to come galloping in among our skirmishers. The officers of companies have always some little exertion to restrain impetuosity, and your galloping gentlemen set our men wild sometimes. We Light Division, while ever conspicuous for undaunted bravery, prided ourselves upon destroying the enemy and preserving ourselves; for good, light troops, like deer-stalkers, may effect feats of heroism by stratagem, ability, and cool daring.

At Tarbes [20 March] we fell in with the enemy, strongly posted, but evidently only a rear-guard in force. The Duke made immediate dispositions to attack them, and so mixed up did we appear, that we concluded a large number of the enemy must be cut off. The Light Division, however, alone succeeded in getting up with them. Our three Battalions of the 95th were most sharply engaged. Three successive times the enemy, with greatly superior force, endeavoured to drive them off a hill but the loss of the enemy from the fire of our Rifles was so great that one could not believe one's eyes. I certainly had never seen the dead lie so thick, nor ever did, except subsequently at Waterloo.

Barnard even asked the Duke to ride over the hill and see the sight, which he consented to do, saying, "Well, Barnard, to please you, I will go, but I require no novel proof of the destructive fire of your Rifles."

At this period we lived capitally. It was delightful to see one of our soldiers with a piece of cold bacon, slicing it over his bread like an English haymaker.

We had at this time exceedingly wet weather. Notwithstanding the fulness of the Garonne, however, after a feint or two and some skilful demonstrations to deceive the enemy, the Duke succeeded [4 April] in throwing over the 3rd, 4th, and 6th Divisions with as much ease as he had previously overcome what seemed to others insurmountable difficulties. These Divisions were strongly posted under Marshal Beresford as a tête du pont. They were barely established on the opposite side when such a torrent of rain fell, our bridge could not stem the flood.

It was hauled to the shore, and, of course, our communication cut off. Marshal Beresford had every reason to apprehend an attack, for the enemy, being in his own country, possessed perfect information, and would know the moment the bridge was impassable.

The Marshal wrote very strongly to the Duke, who was ferried over in a little boat with one or two of his Staff, while their horses swam across.

His Grace quickly but narrowly examined the position, which was excellent, behind a very difficult ravine. "Beresford," said the Duke, "you are safe enough; two such armies as Soult's could make no impression on you. Be assured, he is too clever a General to attempt to drive you into the river."

Our Division was immediately opposite the bridge, but on the left, or opposite bank, to the Marshal. The river soon subsided sufficiently to enable us to relay the bridge, and at daylight on the

10th of April the Light Division crossed, followed by the remainder of the army, except Lord Hill's corps, which was posted on the Pyrenees side of Toulouse. It was evidently the Duke's intention to attack Soult's position this day. Nor were we long on the march before each general officer had his point of rendezvous designated.

The battle of Toulouse [10 April] has been so often fought and refought, I shall only make two or three remarks. Sir Thomas Picton, as usual, attacked when he ought not, and lost men. The Spaniards made three attacks on a very important part of the enemy's position defended by a strong redoubt. The first was a very courageous though unsuccessful attack; the second, a most gallant, heavy, and persevering one, and had my dear old Light Division been pushed forward on the right of the Spaniards in place of remaining inactive, that attack of the Spaniards would have succeeded. I said so at the moment. The third attempt of the Spaniards was naturally, after two such repulses, a very poor one. At this period, about two o'clock in the afternoon, the Duke's Staff began to look grave, and all had some little disaster to report to His Grace, who says, "Ha, by God, this won't do; I must try something else." We then saw the heads of the 4th and 6th Divisions coming into action immediately on the right flank of the enemy, having been conducted to that particular and vulnerable spot by that gallant, able, and accomplished soldier, my dear friend, John Bell, A.Q.M.G., 4th Division.

I must record an anecdote of John. He was mounted on a noble English hunter, but the most violent and difficult horse to manage I ever rode to hounds, and would of course, in a fight, be equally so. This animal knew by the mode in which she was mounted whether her rider was an artist or not, and in a moment would throw her rider down by way of fun. Colonel Achmuty, a noble fellow, would ride John Bell's horse awkwardly, and she would then plunge like a devil, but if ridden, she was as quiet as possible. John Bell had on this horse a very large and high-peaked Hussar saddle, with his cloak strapped on the pique before, a favourite mode of General Robert Craufurd, who indeed gave Bell the identical saddle. Over this pique Craufurd's black muzzle could barely be discovered (he was a short man), so entrenched was he. In conducting their Divisions, the Staff officers moved on small roads through a country intersected by deep and broad ditches full of water. Many of them attempted to ride on the flanks, but no one succeeded but Bell on his fiery horse. At one ditch John Bell was fairly pitched over the pique on to the neck of his horse, a powerful mare six feet high.

"Oh," says John, in telling this story, "Ah, to get there was extraordinary, but wait! The horse tossed up her head, and by some violent exertion pitched me over the pique back again to my saddle."

"Oh, John!" I exclaimed, "how is that possible?" "With that, Harry, I have nothing to do."

But to the fight. The 4th and 6th Divisions were brought up in most gallant style, carrying redoubt after redoubt, which were ably defended by the enemy. It was the heaviest fighting I ever looked at, slow owing to the redoubts. The ground was gained step by step, and so was the battle of Toulouse. Our Cavalry lost a brilliant opportunity of distinguishing themselves and punishing the rearguard of the French.

This battle appeared to me then, and does the more I reflect on it, the only battle the Duke ever fought without a weight of attack and general support. It was no fault of the Duke's. There are fortunate days in war as in other things. Our attacks were commenced by that of the 3rd Division; then came those of the Spaniards, in which the Light Division did not support as the 4th Division supported us at the heights of Vera. Thus, until the afternoon, we literally had done rather worse than nothing. The success of this battle is to be attributed mainly to the 4th and 6th Divisions, but I will ever assert that the second attack was most heavy and energetic, and would have succeeded if my dear old Division had been shoved up. As a whole, the French lost a great number of men and were thoroughly defeated. The French have now agitated a claim to the victory, which they are as much borne out in as they would be in claiming the victory at Waterloo.

The next day [11 March] various were the reports flying about camp as to peace, etc. In the afternoon I was posting a picquet, and in riding forward no nearer than usual to a French sentry, the fellow most deliberately fired at me. I took off my cocked hat and made him a low bow. The fellow, in place of reloading his musket, presented arms to me, evidently ashamed of what he had done.

Peace was soon made known. The French moved out of Toulouse, and we occupied it. (The most slippery pavement to ride over in Europe is that of the streets of Toulouse.) My Division was most comfortably cantoned in the suburbs. I and my wife, and two or three of my dear old Rifle comrades -- Jack Molloy and young Johnstone -- had a delightfully furnished château. We got a French cook, and were as extravagant and wanton in our ideas as lawless sailors just landed from a long cruise. The feeling of no war, no picquets, no alerts, no apprehension of being turned out, was so novel after six years perpetual and vigilant war, it is impossible to describe the sensation. Still, it was one of momentary anxiety, seeing around us the promptitude, the watchfulness, the readiness with which we could move and be in a state of defence or attack. It was so novel that at first it was positively painful -- at least, I can answer for myself in this feeling. I frequently deemed the old Division in danger, who had never even lost a picquet, or, to my recollection, a sentry, after so many years' outpost duty.

We had one melancholy duty to wind up our period of war -- the funeral of poor Colonel Coghlan, 61st Regiment. The officers of the army attended, the Duke himself as chief mourner. Many is the gallant fellow we had all seen left on the field or with some trifling ceremony consigned to his long home; but this funeral, in the midst of a populous city, in a graveyard, after a ceremony in a Protestant chapel, where the corpse was placed, in the custom of our home and infancy, while the service was read by a clergyman, after death in the last battle, and nearly at the end of it, too -- all so tended to excite our comrade-like feelings, it positively depressed us all, for the love a soldier bears another tried and gallant soldier is more than fraternal.

Toulouse, a royalist city, soon rushed into the extravagant and vivacious joy of France. We had theatres, balls, fêtes, etc., until the army moved into regular cantonments. There we had plenty of room and quarters, no squabbling about the shade of a tree in bivouac, or your stable being previously occupied by cavalry or artillery horses. Abundance of food, drink, and raiment, and the indolence of repose, succeeded the energetic and exciting occupation of relentless and cruel war. I had a safeguard in a lovely young wife; but most of our gallant fellows were really in love, or fancied themselves so, and such had been the drain by conscription of the male population, you never saw a young Frenchman. The rich and fertile fields in this part of France were cultivated by female exertion.

My Division went to Castel Sarrasin [towards the end of April]. This place is situated on the Tarne, which divides it from Marsac, where were a body of French troops; but, as they seldom came to visit us, we seldom encroached upon them, for the Napoleonist officers were brutally sulky and so uncivil, John Bull could not put up with it with impunity. This part of France is a garden, and the views, trees, beautiful rivers, and the idleness rendered it a perfect Elysium. I say "idleness;" -- because it was so totally novel, it was amusing. Fortunately -- for we were nine months in arrear of pay -- money was so scarce that a trifle of ready money produced a great deal. Among the rich inhabitants money was never seen, any more than young men. Rents were paid in produce, wages in kind, purchases made by barter.

Chapter 19

Harry Smith parts from his wife before starting for the war in America

My happiness of indolence and repose was doomed to be of short duration, for on the 28th of August I was in the Battle of Bladensburg, and at the capture of the American capital, Washington, some thousands of miles distant. Colborne, my ever dear, considerate friend, then in command of his gallant Corps, the 52nd, sent for me, and said:

"You have been so unlucky, after all your gallant and important service, in not getting your Majority, you must not be idle. There is a force, a considerable one, going to America. You must go. To-morrow we will ride to Toulouse to head-quarters; send a horse on to-night -- it is only thirty-four miles -- we will go there and breakfast, and ride back to dinner."

I said, very gratefully, "Thank you, sir; I will be ready. This is a kind act of yours;" but as I knew I must leave behind my young, fond and devoted wife, my heart was ready to burst, and all my visions for our mutual happiness were banished in search of the bubble reputation. I shall never forget her frenzied grief when, with a sort of despair, I imparted the inevitable separation that we were doomed to suffer, after all our escapes, fatigue, and privation; but a sense of duty surmounted all these domestic feelings, and daylight saw me and dear Colborne full gallop thirty-four miles to breakfast. We were back again at Castel Sarrasin by four in the afternoon, after a little canter of sixty-eight miles, not regarded as any act of prowess, but just a ride. In those days there were men.

On our arrival in Toulouse, we found my name rather high up -- the third, I think -- on the list of Majors of Brigade in the A.G.'s office desirous to serve in America. We asked kind old Darling who had put my name down.

He said, "Colonel Elley," afterwards Sir John.

He had known my family in early life, and was ever paternally kind to me. He had asked my ever dear friend, General Sir Edward Pakenham, to do so, which he readily did.

Colborne then said, "My old friend Ross, who commanded the 20th Regiment while I was Captain of the Light Company, is going. I will go and ask him to take you as his Major of Brigade."

Ross knew me on the retreat to Coruña, and the affair, in a military point of view, was satisfactorily settled. But oh! the heaviness of my heart when I had to impart the separation now decided on to my affectionate young wife of seventeen years old! She bore it, as she did everything, when the energies of her powerful mind were called forth, exclaiming:

"It is for your advantage, and neither of us must repine. All your friends have been so kind in arranging the prospect before you so satisfactorily." At the word "friends" she burst into a flood of tears, which relieved her, exclaiming, "You have friends everywhere. I must be expatriated, separated from relations, go among strangers, while I lose the only thing on earth my life hangs on and clings to!"

Preparation was speedily made for our journey down the Garonne, which we performed in a small boat, accompanied by our kind friend Digby. My wife was to accompany me to Bordeaux, there to embark for England with my brother Tom, who had recently suffered excessively in the extraction of the ball he had received in his knee five years previously at the Coa. The great difficulty I had was to get my regimental pay (nine months being due to me), and I only did so through the kindness of our acting-paymaster, Captain Stewart, and every officer readily saying, "Oh, give us so much less the first issue, and let Smith have what would otherwise come to us." Such an act, I say, testifies to the mutual friendship and liberality we acquired amidst scenes of glory, hardship, and privation.

Before I left my old Brigade, the 52nd Regiment, the 95th Regiment (Rifle Brigade now), the 1st and 3rd Caçadores, with whom I had been so many eventful years associated -- and I may say, most happily -- all gave me a parting dinner, including the good fellows, the Portuguese, whom I never had any chance of seeing again. Our farewell dinner partook of every feeling of excitement. The private soldiers, too, were most affectionate, and I separated from all as from my home. The Portuguese are a brave, kind-hearted people, and most susceptible of kindness. We had also ten men a Company in our British Regiments, Spaniards, many of them the most daring of sharpshooters in our corps, who nobly regained the distinction attached to the name of the Spanish infantry in Charles V.'s time. I never saw better, more orderly, perfectly sober soldiers in my life, and as vedettes the old German Hussar did not exceed them. The 52nd Regiment I was as much attached to as my own corps, with every reason.

My old 1st Battalion embarked at Dover just before Talavera, 1050 rank and file. During the war only 100 men joined us. We were now reduced to about 500. There was scarcely a man who had not been wounded. There was scarcely one whose knowledge of his duty as an outpost soldier was not brought to a state of perfection, and when they were told they must not drink, a drunken man was a rare occurence indeed, as rare as a sober one when we dare give a little latitude. My old Brigade was equal to turn the tide of victory (as it did at Orthez) any day.

It was early in May when we left Castel Sarrasin, where we had been happy (oh, most happy!) for a month -- an age in the erratic life we had been leading. We were quartered in the house of a Madame La Rivière, an excellent and motherly woman, a widow with a large family and only one son spared to her -- the rest had perished as soldiers. Never was there a more happy and cheerful family, and never did mother endeavour to soothe the acute feelings of a daughter more than did this good lady those of my poor wife. We often afterwards heard of her in Paris in 1815.

Our voyage down the Garonne in our little skiff was delightful. We anchored every night. In youth everything is novel and exciting, and our voyage was such a change after marching! The beauties of the scenery, and the drooping foliage on the banks of the river, added to our enjoyment. We landed each night at some town or village, and ever found a comfortable inn which could give us a dinner. After such privations as ours, the delight of being able to order dinner at an inn is not to be believed.

On reaching Bordeaux, the most beautiful city I was ever in, I found I had only three or four days to prepare to reach the fleet, and that I was to embark on board his Majesty's ship the *Royal Oak*, for the troops under General Ross were destined for a peculiar and separate service in America.

I did, of course, all I could to draw the attention of my poor wife from the approaching separation. There was a theatre, various spectacles, sights, etc., but all endeavour was vain to relieve the mind one instant from the awful thought of that one word "separation." Digby was most kind to her. He had an excellent private servant, who was to embark with her for London. My brother Tom was to her all a brother could be, and in the transport she was to proceed in were several old and dear Rifle friends going to England from wounds. I wished her to go to London for some time before going down to my father's, for the benefit of masters to learn English, etc. -- for not a word could she speak but her own language, French, and Portuguese, -- and to every wish she readily assented.

Time rolls rapidly on to the goal of grief, and the afternoon arrived when I must ride twenty miles on my road for embarcation. Many a year has now gone by, still the recollection of that afternoon is as fresh in my memory as it was painful at the moment. I left her insensible and in a faint. God only knows the number of staggering and appalling dangers I had faced; but, thank the Almighty, I never was unmanned until now, and I leaped on my horse by that impulse which guides the soldier to do his duty.

I had a long ride before me on the noble mare destined to embark with me. On my way I reached a village where I received the attention of a kind old lady, who from her age had been exempt from having any troops quartered on her; but, the village being full of Rifle Brigade, Artillery, and Light Division fellows, the poor old lady was saddled with me. The Artillery readily took charge of my horse. The kind old grandmamma showed me into a neat little bedroom and left me. I threw myself on the bed as one alone in all the wide world, a feeling never before experienced, when my eye caught some prints on the wall. What should they be but pictures in representation of the Sorrows of Werther, and, strange though it be, they had the contrary effect upon me to that which at the first glance I anticipated. They roused me from my sort of lethargy of grief and inspired a hope which never after abandoned me. The good lady had a nice little supper of côtelettes de mouton, and the most beautiful strawberries I ever saw, and she opened a bottle of excellent wine. To gratify her I swallowed by force all I could, for her kindness was maternal.

We soon parted for ever, for I was on horseback before daylight, en route to Pauillac, a village on the Garonne, where we were to embark. On my ride, just at grey daylight, I saw something walking in the air.

"It is like a man," I said, "certainly, only that men do not walk in the air."

It advanced towards me with apparently rapid strides, and in the excited state of mind I was in, I really believed I was deluded, and ought not to believe what I saw. Suspense was intolerable, and I galloped up to it. As I neared my aeronaut, I found it a man walking on stilts about twenty-five feet high. In the imperfect light and the distance, of course the stilts were invisible. The phenomenon was accounted for, and my momentary credulity in I did not know what called to mind stories I had heard recounted, evidently the results heated imaginations. This walking on stilts is very general in the deep sands of this country.

On reaching Pauillac, I found my trusty old groom West waiting for me. He led me to a comfortable billet, where my portmanteau, all my worldly property, and my second horse, which was to embark with me, were reported

"All right, sir."

Old West did not ask after "Mrs.," but he looked at me a thousand inquiries, to which I shook my head. I found a note for me at our military post-office from dear little Digby, as consolatory as I could expect.

I was detained two days at Pauillac, in the house of another widow, an elderly lady (all women in France of moderate or certain age were widows at this period). One morning I heard a most extraordinary shout of joyful exclamation, so much so I ran into the room adjoining the one I was sitting in.

The poor old woman says, "Oh, come in and witness my happiness!" She was locked in the arms of a big, stout-looking, well-whiskered Frenchman. "Here is my son, oh! my long-lost son, who has been a prisoner in England from the beginning of the war."

The poor fellow was a sous-officier in a man-of-war, and, having been taken early in the war off Boulogne, for years he had been in those accursed monsters of inhuman invention, "the hulks," a prisoner. He made no complaint. He said England had no other place to keep their prisoners, that they were well fed when fed by the English, but when, by an arrangement with France at her own request, that Government fed them, they were half starved. The widow gave a great dinner-party at two o'clock, to which I was of course invited.

The poor old lady said, "Now let us drink some of this wine: it was made the year my poor son was taken prisoner. I vowed it should never be opened until he was restored to me, and this day I have broached the cask." The wine was excellent. If all the wine-growers had sons taken prisoners, and kept it thus until their release, the world would be well supplied with good wine in place of bad. Poor family! it was delightful to witness their happiness, while I could but meditate on the contrast between it and my wretchedness. But I lived in hope.

That afternoon, after seeing my horses off; I embarked in a boat, and I and all my personal property, my one portmanteau, reached the *Royal Oak*, at her anchorage a few miles below, about eight o'clock.

[Here there is a break in this narrative where it turns to Smith's service in America. The following chapter begins with his return to England at the time of Napoleon's escape from Elba.]

Chapter 20

Harry Smith returns to England

As we neared the mouth of the British Channel, we had, of course, the usual thick weather, when a strange sail was reported. It was now blowing a fresh breeze; in a few minutes we spoke her, but did not make her haul her main-topsail, being a bit of a merchantman. Stirling hailed as we shot past.

"Where are you from?"

"Portsmouth."

"Any news?"

"No, none." The ship was almost out of sight, when we heard:

"Ho! Bonaparter's back again on the throne of France." Such a hurrah as I set up, tossing my hat over my head!

"I will be a Lieutenant-Colonel yet before the year's out!"

Sir John Lambert said, "Really, Smith, you are so vivacious! How is it possible? It cannot be." He had such faith in the arrangements of our government, he wouldn't believe it.

I said, "Depend upon it, it's truth; a beast like that skipper never could have invented it, when he did not even regard it as news: 'No, no news; only Bonaparte's back again on the throne of France.' Depend on it, it's true."

"No, Smith, no." Stirling believed it, and oh, how he carried on!

We were soon at Spithead, when all the men-of-war, the bustle, the general appearance, told us, before we could either see telegraphic communication or speak any one, where "Bonaparter" was.

We anchored about three o'clock, went on shore immediately, and shortly after were at dinner in the George. Old West had brought from the Havannah two pups of little white curly dogs, a dog and bitch, which he said were "a present for missus." They are very much esteemed in England, these Havana lapdogs; not much in my way.

The charm of novelty which I experienced on my former visit to England after seven years absence, was much worn off; and I thought of nothing but home. Sir John and I started for London in a chaise at night, and got only as far as Guildford. I soon found our rate of progression would not do, and I asked his leave to set off home. At that time he was not aware of all my tale. I never saw his affectionate heart angry before; he positively scolded me, and said, "I will report our arrival; write to me, that I may know your address, for I shall most probably very soon want you again." My wife and Sir John were afterwards the greatest friends.

So Mr. West and I got a chaise, and off we started, and got to London on a Sunday, the most melancholy place on that day on earth. I drove to my old lodgings, where I had last parted from my wife. They could assure me she was well, as she had very lately ordered a new riding-habit. So I ordered a post-chaise and ran from Panton Square to Weeks' in the Haymarket, and bought a superb dressing-case and a heavy gold chain; I had brought a lot of Spanish books from the Havannah. So on this occasion I did not return to my home naked and penniless, as from Coruña.

I got to Waltham Cross about twelve o'clock. I soon found a pair of horses was far too slow for my galloping ideas; so I got four, and we galloped along then as fast as I could wish. I rattled away to the Falcon Inn in my native place, Whittlesea; for I dare not drive to my father's house. I sent quietly for him, and he was with me in a moment. The people were in church as I drove past. My wife was there, so as yet she was safe from any sudden alarm. She and my sisters took a walk after church, when servants were sent in every direction in search of them, with orders quietly to say that my father wanted my sisters. A fool of a fellow being the first to find them, and delighted with his prowess, ran up, shouting, "Come home directly; a gentleman has come in a chaise-and-four" -- who, he did not know. My poor wife, as he named no one, immediately believed some one had arrived to say I was killed, and down she fell senseless. My sisters soon restored her, and they ran home, to their delight, into my arms.

We were now all happiness. During my few months' absence

nothing had occurred to damp their contentment; so we all blessed God Almighty that I had again been protected in such awful situations both by land and sea, while so many families had to grieve for the loss of their dearest relatives. Pug and Tiny recognized me. I heard from Sir John Lambert that he was to be employed with the army assembling at Brussels under the Duke, that I had better be prepared to join him at a few hours' notice, that my position near him would require horses. I knew that "Major of Brigade" was the berth intended for me. My wife was to accompany me again to the war, but nothing affected us when united; the word "separation" away, all was smooth. All was now excitement, joy, hope and animation, and preparation of riding-habits, tents, canteens, etc., my sisters thinking of all sorts of things for my wife's comfort, which we could as well have carried as our parish church. My youngest brother but one, Charles, was to go with me to join the 1st Battalion Rifle Brigade, as a Volunteer, and his departure added to the excitement. I never was more happy in all my life; not a thought of the future (though God knows we had enough before us), for my wife was going and all the agony of parting was spared.

I immediately set to work to buy a real good stud. Two horses I bought at Newmarket, and two in my native place; and as Tiny the faithful was voted too old, as was the mare I had with me in Spain and Washington, I bought for my wife, from a brother, a mare of great celebrity, bred by my father, a perfect horse for a lady who was an equestrian artist.

In a few days I had a kind letter from Sir John Lambert, saying I was appointed his Major of Brigade; and as he was to proceed to Ghent in Flanders, recommending me, being in Cambridgeshire, to proceed viâ Harwich for Ostend, as I must find my own passage unless I went on a transport. West was therefore despatched with my four horses viâ Newmarket for Harwich, and I intended so to start as to be there the day my horses would arrive.

The evening before we started, my father, wife, sisters, myself, and brothers had a long ride. On returning, at the end of the town, there was a new stiff rail, with a ditch on each side. I was riding my dear old mare, that had been at Washington, etc., and off whose back poor Lindsay had been killed; she was an elegant fencer, and as bold as in battle. I said to my sisters, "I will have one more leap on my war-horse." I rode her at it. Whether she had grown old, or did not measure her leap, I don't know, but over she rolled. One of my legs was across the new and narrow ditch, her shoulder right upon it; I could not pull it from under her. I expected every moment, if she struggled, to feel my leg broken, and there was an end to my Brigade Majorship! I passed a hand down, until I got short hold of the curb, and gave her a snatch with all my force. She made an effort, and I drew my leg out, more faint than subsequently in the most sanguinary conflict of the whole war. I never felt more grateful for an escape.

Chapter 21

The Waterloo Campaign -- Ghent -- Battle of Waterloo

My wife and I and my brother Charles were to start in a chaise at three o'clock the next morning. I never saw my poor father suffer so much as at thus parting from three of us at once, and feeling that his companion, my wife, was lost to him. He said, "Napoleon and Wellington will meet, a battle will ensue of a kind never before heard of, and I cannot expect to see you all again."

We reached Harwich in the afternoon, found West, his horses, and all our things right, and went to the Black Bull, from whence I had embarked years before for Gottenburgh. There we found my old acquaintance, the landlord, Mr. Briton, a man as civil as full of information. He said I had no chance of embarking at Harwich, unless I freighted a small craft that he would look out, and fitted it up for my horses.

Next day I came to terms with the skipper of a sloop of a few tons' burden, himself and a boy the crew. I couldn't help thinking of the 74's and frigates in which I had been flying over the ocean. We measured it, and found there was just room for the horses, and a hole aft, called a cabin, for my wife and self and brother. I did not intend to embark the horses till the wind was fair–a fortunate plan, for I was detained in the Black Bull by foul winds for a fortnight. The wind becoming fair, in the afternoon we embarked all our traps. Mr. Briton amply provided us with provisions and forage, and brought his bill for myself, wife, brother, two grooms, five horses, lady's maid, sea stock, etc. I expected it to be fifty or sixty pounds; it was twenty-four and some shillings, and we had lived on the fat of the land, for having been half-starved so many years, when once in the flesh-pots of England, we revelled in a plenty which we could scarcely fancy would last.

A gentle breeze carried us over to Ostend in twenty-four hours, where we landed our horses by slinging them and dropping them into the sea to swim ashore. My wife's noble mare, which we called the "Brass Mare" after her son of that ilk, when in the slings and in sight of the shore, neighed most gallantly, and my wife declared it an omen of brilliant success. We went to the great inn of Ostend. The difference between it and our late bivouac, the Black Bull, is not to be described. I found an English horse-dealer there. I bought two mules of him and a stout Flanders pony for our baggage, and in three days we were en route for Ghent, stopping one night at Bruges, where was an excellent inn, and the best Burgundy I had drunk up to that hour. My wife was delighted to be once more in campaigning trim.

When we reached Ghent we found Sir John Lambert had reached it the day before. Louis XVIII. was there, his Court and idlers, and Ghent was in as great a state of excitement as if the Duke of Marlborough was again approaching. I found our Brigade were all New Orleans Regiments—three of the best regiments of the old Army of the Peninsula, the 4th, 27th, and 40th, and the 81st in garrison at Brussels. We were ordered to be in perfect readiness to take the field with the warning we had been so many years accustomed to.

Louis held a Court while we were there. I was near the door he entered by. He was very inactive, but impressive in manner. He laid his hand on my shoulder to support himself. His great topic of conversation was how delighted he was to see us, and how much he was indebted to our nation. A more benign countenance I never beheld, nor did his subsequent reign belie the benignity of his expression.

While at Ghent I waited on Sir John Lambert every morning just after breakfast for orders.

On one occasion we heard a voice thundering in the passage to him, "Hallo there, where the devil's the door?" I went out, and to my astonishment saw our noble friend Admiral Malcolm. "Why, where the devil has Lambert stowed himself? The house is as dark as a sheer hulk." He was delighted to see us, and sang out, "Come, bear a hand and get me some breakfast; no regular hours on shore as in the *Royal Oak*."

He had been appointed to the command of the coast. He was

very much attached to the Duke. During our stay at Ghent we had Brigade parades almost every day, and my General, an ex-Adjutant of the Guards, was most particular in all guard mountings, sentries, and all the correct minutiæ of garrison. The three regiments were in beautiful fighting trim, although the headquarters ship with the Grenadiers, the 27th, had not arrived from America. Poor 27th! in a few days they had not two hundred men in the ranks.

As we anticipated, our march from Ghent was very sudden. In an hour after the order arrived we moved en route for Brussels. We reached Asche on the afternoon of the 16th June. The rapid and continuous firing at Quatre Bras, as audible as if we were in the fight, put us in mind of old times, as well as on the qui vive. We expected an order every moment to move on. We believed the firing to be at Fleurus. As we approached Brussels the next day [17 June], we met an orderly with a letter from that gallant fellow De Lancey, Q.M.G., to direct us to move on Quatre Bras.

In the afternoon, after we passed Brussels, the scene of confusion, the flying of army, baggage, etc., was an awful novelty to us. We were directed by a subsequent order to halt at the village of Epinay, on the Brussels side of the forest of Soignies, a report having reached his Grace that the enemy's cavalry were threatening our communication with Brussels (as we understood, at least). The whole afternoon we were in a continued state of excitement.

Once some rascals of the Cumberland Hussars, a new Corps of Hanoverians (not of the style of our noble and gallant old comrades, the 1st Hussars), came galloping in, declaring they were pursued by Frenchmen. Our bugles were blowing in all directions, and our troops running to their alarm-posts in front of the village. I went to report to Sir John Lambert, who was just sitting quietly down to dinner with my wife and his A.D.C.

He says very coolly, "Let the troops --; this is all nonsense; there is not a French soldier in the rear of his Grace, depend on it, and sit down to dinner."

I set off; though, and galloped to the front, where a long line of baggage was leisurely retiring. This was a sufficient indication that the alarm was false, and I dismissed the troops and started for the débris of a magnificent turbot which the General's butler had brought out of Brussels. This was in the afternoon.

Such a thunderstorm and deluge of rain now came on, it drenched all that was exposed to it, and in a few minutes rendered the country deep in mud and the roads very bad. All night our baggage kept retiring through the village.

In the course of the night, Lambert's Brigade were ordered to move up to the position the Duke had taken up in front of the forest of Soignies, and our march was very much impeded by waggons upset, baggage thrown down, etc. [18 June]. We met Sir George Scovell, an A.Q.M.G. at head-quarters, who said he was sent by the Duke to see the rear was clear, that it was choked between this and the Army, and the Duke expected to be attacked immediately; our Brigade must clear the road before we moved on. Our men were on fire at the idea of having to remain and clear a road when an attack was momentarily expected, and an hour would bring us to the position. The wand of a magician, with all his spells and incantations, could not have effected a clear course sooner than our 3000 soldiers of the old school.

This effected, General Lambert sent me on to the Duke for orders. I was to find the Duke himself, and receive orders from no other person. About 11 o'clock I found his Grace and all his staff near Hougoumont. The day was beautiful after the storm, although the country was very heavy.

When I rode up, he said, "Hallo, Smith, where are you from last?"

"From General Lambert's Brigade, and they from America."

"What have you got?"

"The 4th, the 27th, and the 40th; the 81st remain in Brussels."

"Ah, I know, I know; but the others, are they in good order?"

"Excellent, my lord, and very strong."

"That's all right, for I shall soon want every man."

One of his staff said, "I do not think they will attack to-day."

"Nonsense," said the Duke. "The columns are already forming, and I think I have discerned where the weight of the attack will be made. I shall be attacked before an hour. Do you know anything of my position, Smith?"

"Nothing, my lord, beyond what I see -- the general line, and right and left."

"Go back and halt Lambert's Brigade at the junction of the two great roads from Genappe and Nivelles. Did you observe their junction as you rode up?"

"Particularly, my lord."

"Having halted the head of the Brigade and told Lambert what I desire, ride to the left of the position. On the extreme left is the Nassau Brigade—those fellows who came over to us at Arbonne, you recollect. Between them and Picton's Division (now the 5th) I shall most probably require Lambert. There is already there a Brigade of newly-raised Hanoverians, which Lambert will give orders to, as they and your Brigade form the 6th Division. You are the only British Staff Officer with it. Find out, therefore, the best and shortest road from where Lambert is now halted to the left of Picton and the right of the Nassau troops. Do you understand?"

"Perfectly, my lord." I had barely turned from his Grace when he called me back.

"Now, clearly understand that when Lambert is ordered to move from the fork of the two roads where he is now halted, you are prepared to conduct him to Picton's left."

It was delightful to see his Grace that morning on his noble horse Copenhagen—in high spirits and very animated, but so cool and so clear in the issue of his orders, it was impossible not fully to comprehend what he said; delightful also to observe what his wonderful eye anticipated, while some of his staff were of opinion the attack was not in progress.

I had hardly got back to Lambert, after reconnoitring the country and preparing myself to conduct the troops, when the Battle of Waterloo commenced.

We soon saw that where we should be moved to, the weight of the attack on Picton would be resisted by none but British soldiers. For a few seconds, while every regiment was forming square, and the charge of Ponsonby's Brigade going on (which the rising ground in our front prevented us seeing), it looked as if the formation was preparatory to a retreat. Many of the rabble of Dutch troops were flying towards us, and, to add to the confusion, soon after came a party of dragoons, bringing with them three eagles and some prisoners.

I said to General Lambert, "We shall have a proper brush immediately, for it looks as if our left will be immediately turned, and the brunt of the charge will fall on us."

At this moment we were ordered to move to the very spot where the Duke, early in the morning, had expected we should be required. Picton had been killed, Sir James Kempt commanded on the left of the road to Genappe, near La Haye Sainte; his Division had been already severely handled, and we took their position, my old Battalion of Riflemen remaining with us.

The Battle of Waterloo has been too often described, and nonsense enough written about the Crisis, for me to add to it. Every moment was a crisis, and the controversialists had better have left the discussion on the battle-field. Every Staff officer had two or three (and one four) horses shot under him. I had one wounded in six, another in seven places, but not seriously injured. The fire was terrific, especially of cannon.

Late in the day, when the enemy had made his last great effort on our centre, the field was so enveloped in smoke that nothing was discernible. The firing ceased on both sides, and we on the left knew that one party or the other was beaten. This was the most anxious moment of my life. In a few seconds we saw the red-coats in the centre, as stiff as rocks, and the French columns retiring rapidly, and there was such a British shout as rent the air. We all felt then to whom the day belonged. It was time the "Crisis" should arrive, for we had been at work some hours, and the hand of death had been most unsparing. One Regiment, the 27th had only two officers left–Major Hume, who commanded from the beginning of the battle, and another–and they were both wounded, and only a hundred and twenty soldiers were left with them.

At this moment I saw the Duke, with only one Staff officer remaining, galloping furiously to the left. I rode on to meet him.

"Who commands here?"

"Generals Kempt and Lambert, my lord."

"Desire them to get into a column of companies of Battalions, and move on immediately."

I said, "In which direction, my lord?"

"Right ahead, to be sure." I never saw his Grace so animated. The Crisis was general, from one end of the line to the other.

That evening at dark we halted, literally on the ground we stood on; not a picquet was required, and our whole cavalry in pursuit. Then came the dreadful tale of killed and wounded; it was enormous, and every moment the loss of a dear friend was announced. To my wonder, my astonishment, and to my gratitude to Almighty God, I and my two brothers -- Tom, the Adjutant of the 2nd Battalion Rifle Brigade, who had, during the day, attracted the Duke's attention by his gallantry, and Charles, in the 1st Battalion, who had been fighting for two days -- were all safe and unhurt, except that Charles had a slight wound in the neck. In the thunderstorm the previous evening he had tied a large silk handkerchief over his stock; he forgot to take it off; and probably owed his life to so trifling a circumstance.

There was not an instance throughout the Army of two brothers in the field escaping. We were three, and I could hardly credit my own eyes. We had nothing to eat or drink. I had some tea in my writing-case, but no sugar. It had been carried by an orderly, although in the ranks. He found me out after the battle, and I made some tea in a soldier's tin for Sir James Kempt, Sir John Lambert, and myself; and while we were thus regaling, up came my brother, of whose safety I was not aware.

Captain McCulloch of the 95th Regiment wished to see me. He was a dear friend whom I had not seen since he was awfully wounded at Foz de Aronce on Massena's retreat, after having had seven sabre-wounds at the Coa, in Massena's advance, and been taken prisoner. He was in a cottage near, awfully wounded. I found him lying in great agony, but very composed.

"Oh, Harry, so long since we have met, and now again under such painful circumstances; but, thank God, you and Tom are all right."

I had brought all my remaining tea, which he ravenously swallowed. The ball had dreadfully broken the elbow of the sound arm, and had passed right through the fleshy part of his back, while the broken bone of the arm previously shattered at Foz de Aronce was still exfoliating, and very painful even after a lapse of years. I got hold of a surgeon, and his arm was immediately amputated. When dressed, he lay upon the stump, as this was less painful than the old exfoliating wound, and on his back he could not lie. He recovered, but was never afterwards able to feed himself or put on his hat, and died, Heaven help him, suddenly of dysentery.

No one, but those who have witnessed the awful scene, knows the horrors of a field of battle -- the piles of the dead, the groans of the dying, the agony of those dreadfully wounded, to whom frequently no assistance can be rendered at the moment; some still in perfect possession of their intellect, game to the last, regarding their recovery as more than probable, while the clammy perspiration of death has already pounced upon its victim; others, again, perfectly sensible of their dissolution, breathing into your keeping the feelings and expressions of their last moments -- messages to father, mother, wife, or dearest relatives.

Often have I myself, tired and exhausted in such scenes, almost regretted the life I have adopted, in which one never knows at any moment how near or distant one's own turn may be. In such dejection you sink into a profound sleep, and you stand up next morning in fresh spirits. Your country's calls, your excitement, honour and glory, again impel, and undauntedly and cheerfully you expose that life which the night before you fancied was of value. A soldier's life is one continued scene of excitement, hope, anticipation; fear for himself he never knows, though the loss of his comrade pierces his heart.

Before daylight next morning [19 June] a Staff officer whose name I now forget, rode up to where we were all lying, and told us of the complete déroute of the French, and the vigorous pursuit of the Prussians, and that it was probable that our Division would not move for some hours. At daylight I was on horseback, with a heart of gratitude as became me, and anxious to let my wife know I was all right. I took a party of each Regiment of my Division with me, and went back to the field; for I was now established as Assistant-Quartermaster-General.

I had been over many a field of battle, but with the exception of one spot at New Orleans, and the breach of Badajos, I had never seen anything to be compared with what I saw. At Waterloo the whole field from right to left was a mass of dead bodies. In one spot, to the right of La Haye Sainte, the French Cuirassiers were literally piled on each other; many soldiers not wounded lying under their horses; others, fearfully wounded, occasionally with their horses struggling upon their wounded bodies. The sight was sickening, and I had no means or power to assist them.

Imperative duty compelled me to the field of my comrades, where I had plenty to do to assist many who had been left out all night; some had been believed to be dead, but the spark of life had returned. All over the field you saw officers, and as many soldiers as were permitted to leave the ranks, leaning and weeping over some dead or dying brother or comrade. The battle was fought on a Sunday, the 18th June, and I repeated to myself a verse from the Psalms of that day—91st Psalm, 7th verse: "A thousand shall fall beside thee, and ten thousand at thy right hand, but it shall not come nigh thee." I blessed Almighty God our Duke was spared, and galloped to my General, whom I found with some breakfast awaiting my arrival.

So many accounts and descriptions have been given of the Battle of Waterloo, I shall only make one or two observations. To those who say the ultimate success of the day was achieved by the arrival of the Prussians, I observe that the Prussians were part of the whole on which his Grace calculated, as much as on the co-operation of one of his own Divisions; that they ought to have been in the field much sooner, and by their late arrival seriously endangered his Grace's left flank; and had Napoleon pushed the weight of his attack and precipitated irresistible numbers on our left, he would have forced the Duke to throw back his left and break our communication with the Prussians. The Duke's army was a heterogeneous mass, not the old Peninsular veterans; young 2nd Battalions most of them, others intermixed with the rabble of our allied army. Thus the Duke could not have counter-manoeuvred on his left, as he would have been able with his old army; and we had one Division under Colville far away to our right.

Napoleon fought the battle badly; his attacks were not simultaneous, but partial and isolated, and enabled the Duke to repel each by a concentration. His cavalry was sacrificed early in the day. If Napoleon did not desire to turn our left flank, and the battle is to be regarded as a fight hand to hand, he fought it badly.

By a general attack upon our line with his overpowering force of artillery, followed up by his infantry, he might have put hors-de-combat far more of our army than he did. His cavalry would have been fresh, and had he employed this devoted and gallant auxiliary late in the day as he did early, his attempts to defeat us would have been far more formidable.

His artillery and cavalry behaved most nobly, but I maintain his infantry did not. In proof, I will record one example.

On the left, in front of the 5th Division, 25,000 of the Young Guard attacked in column. Picton was just killed, and Kempt commanded. It is true this column advanced under a galling fire, but it succeeded in reaching the spot where it intended to deploy. Kempt ordered the Battalion immediately opposite the head of the column to charge. It was a poor miserable Battalion compared with some of ours, yet did it dash like British soldiers at the column, which went about. Then it was that Ponsonby's Brigade got in among them, and took eagles and prisoners.

As a battle of science, it was demonstrative of no manoeuvre. It was no Salamanca or Vittoria, where science was so beautifully exemplified: it was as a stand-up fight between two pugilists, "mill away" till one is beaten. The Battle of Waterloo, with all its political glory, has destroyed the field movement of the British Army, so scientifically laid down by Dundas, so improved on by that hero of war and of drill, Sir John Moore. All that light-troop duty which he taught, by which the world through the medium of the Spanish War was saved, is now replaced by the most heavy of manoeuvres, by squares, centre formations, and moving in masses, which require time to collect and equal time to extend; and all because the Prussians and Russians did not know how to move quicker, we, forsooth, must adopt their ways, although Picton's Division at Quatre Bras nobly showed that British infantry can resist cavalry in any shape.

It is true the Buffs were awfully mauled at Albuera, but what did my kind patron, Sir William Stewart, order them to do? They were in open column of companies right in front, and it was necessary at once to deploy into line, which Sir William with his light 95th had been accustomed to do on any company: he orders them, therefore, to deploy on the Grenadiers; by this the right would become the left, what in common parlance is termed "clubbed;" and while he was doing this, he kept advancing the Grenadiers. It is impossible to imagine a battalion in a more helpless position, and it never can be cited as any criterion that a battalion must be in squares to resist cavalry.

At the Battle of Fuentes d'Oñoro, the overwhelming French cavalry, having rapidly put back our very inferior force, were upon a regiment of infantry of the 7th Division, to the right of the Light Division, before either were aware. The French advance of the Chasseurs Britanniques, I think (it was one of the mongrels, as we called those corps, anyhow), was imposing, heavy, and rapid (I was close to the left of our infantry at the time), but it made not the slightest impression on the regiment in line; on the contrary, the Chasseurs were repulsed with facility and loss.

But to return to our narrative. A party was sent to bury the dead of each regiment as far as possible. For the Rifle Brigade, my brother Charles was for the duty. In gathering the dead bodies, he saw among the dead of our soldiers the body of a French officer of delicate mould and appearance. On examining it, he found it was that of a delicate, young and handsome female. My story ends here, but such is the fact. What were the circumstances of devotion, passion, or patriotism which led to such heroism, is, and ever will be, to me a mystery. Love, depend upon it.

ALSO FROM LEONAUR
AVAILABLE IN SOFTCOVER OR HARDCOVER WITH DUST JACKET

EW2 EYEWITNESS TO WAR SERIES
CAPTAIN OF THE 95th (Rifles) by Jonathan Leach

An officer of Wellington's Sharpshooters during the Peninsular, South of France and Waterloo Campaigns of the Napoleonic Wars.

SOFTCOVER : **ISBN 1-84677-001-7**
HARDCOVER : **ISBN 1-84677-016-5**

WF1 THE WARFARE FICTION SERIES
NAPOLEONIC WAR STORIES
by Sir Arthur Quiller-Couch

Tales of soldiers, spies, battles & Sieges from the Peninsular & Waterloo campaigns

SOFTCOVER : **ISBN 1-84677-003-3**
HARDCOVER : **ISBN 1-84677-014-9**

EW1 EYEWITNESS TO WAR SERIES
RIFLEMAN COSTELLO by Edward Costello

The adventures of a soldier of the 95th (Rifles) in the Peninsular & Waterloo Campaigns of the Napoleonic wars.

SOFTCOVER : **ISBN 1-84677-000-9**
HARDCOVER : **ISBN 1-84677-018-1**

MC1 THE MILITARY COMMANDERS SERIES
JOURNALS OF ROBERT ROGERS OF THE RANGERS by Robert Rogers

The exploits of Rogers & the Rangers in his own words during 1755-1761 in the French & Indian War.

SOFTCOVER : **ISBN 1-84677-002-5**
HARDCOVER : **ISBN 1-84677-010-6**

AVAILABLE ONLINE AT
www.leonaur.com
AND OTHER GOOD BOOK STORES

ALSO FROM LEONAUR
AVAILABLE IN SOFTCOVER OR HARDCOVER WITH DUST JACKET

RGW1 RECOLLECTIONS OF THE GREAT WAR 1914 - 18
STEEL CHARIOTS IN THE DESERT by S. C. Rolls

The first world war experiences of a Rolls Royce armoured car driver with the Duke of Westminster in Libya and in Arabia with T.E. Lawrence.

SOFTCOVER : **ISBN 1-84677-005-X**
HARDCOVER : **ISBN 1-84677-019-X**

RGW2 RECOLLECTIONS OF THE GREAT WAR 1914 - 18
WITH THE IMPERIAL CAMEL CORPS IN THE GREAT WAR by Geoffrey Inchbald

The story of a serving officer with the British 2nd battalion against the Senussi and during the Palestine campaign.

SOFTCOVER : **ISBN 1-84677-007-6**
HARDCOVER : **ISBN 1-84677-012-2**

EW3 EYEWITNESS TO WAR SERIES
THE KHAKEE RESSALAH
by Robert Henry Wallace Dunlop

Service & adventure with the Meerut Volunteer Horse During the Indian Mutiny 1857-1858.

SOFTCOVER : **ISBN 1-84677-009-2**
HARDCOVER : **ISBN 1-84677-017-3**

WF1 THE WARFARE FICTION SERIES
NAPOLEONIC WAR STORIES
by Sir Arthur Quiller-Couch

Tales of soldiers, spies, battles & Sieges from the Peninsular & Waterloo campaigns

SOFTCOVER : **ISBN 1-84677-003-3**
HARDCOVER : **ISBN 1-84677-014-9**

AVAILABLE ONLINE AT
www.leonaur.com
AND OTHER GOOD BOOK STORES